The Effective Museum

The Effective Museum

Rethinking Museum Practices to Increase Impact

JOHN W. JACOBSEN

ROWMAN & LITTLEFIELD
Lanham • Boulder • New York • London

Published by Rowman & Littlefield
An imprint of The Rowman & Littlefield Publishing Group, Inc.
4501 Forbes Boulevard, Suite 200, Lanham, Maryland 20706
www.rowman.com

86-90 Paul Street, London EC2A 4NE

Cover: The entrance lobby of the Peabody Essex Museum (Salem MA), designed by Moshe Safdie. Photo: John W. Jacobsen

British Library Cataloguing in Publication Information Available

Library of Congress Cataloging-in-Publication Data Available

ISBN 978-1-5381-6434-1 (cloth)
ISBN 978-1-5381-6435-8 (paper)
ISBN 978-1-5381-6436-5 (electronic)

∞™ The paper used in this publication meets the minimum requirements of American National Standard for Information Sciences—Permanence of Paper for Printed Library Materials, ANSI/NISO Z39.48-1992.

This book is dedicated to seven museum leaders and visionaries: Ford Bell, Al DeSena, Alan Friedman, Elaine Gurian, Roger L. Nichols, Roy Shafer, and Stephen Weil. You were my professional mentors, truthsayers, and role models, and your passions for museums inspired this book.

Contents

Acknowledgments

The museum field has passionate and articulate writers and thinkers, and I am indebted to all who write and speak out thoughtfully about museum purposes and values. I am particularly grateful to those who have contributed to my evolving thinking during five decades of collaborations on museum projects. The list of these inspirational colleagues is extensive and included in my previous books.

For this book, I am grateful to the friends and colleagues who spent time reading chapter drafts and commenting on them so thoughtfully. Whatever good qualities this book has, I credit to the edits and suggestions from museum professionals Joe Ansel, Nancy Perkins Arata, Larry Bell, Lynn Baum, Al DeSena, David Ellis, George Hein, Chuck Howarth, Duane Kocik, Mary Maher, Bill Peters, Richard Rabinowitz, Jim Richerson, Laura B. Roberts, Marsha Semmel, Jeanie Stahl, and Robert (Mac) West. Thank you, colleagues, your guidance and insight shed light on my path.

Thanks also to Charles Harmon, Erinn Slanina, and Linda Kessler at Rowman & Littlefield for their editorial and publication support.

I caught my love for museums from four museum mentors who may be gone but are certainly not forgotten: Roger Nichols, the director of the Museum of Science and my boss during one of the museum's most vibrant and successful eras; Roy Shafer, the museum director who went on to coach museums to develop their "conceptual frameworks;" Alan Friedman, the committed museum educator who led by the example of his principled character and brilliance; and Stephen Weil, whose writings underlie all contemporary assumptions about museums and their contributions and effectiveness. I am also motivated by Ford Bell's advocacy, when he led the American Alliance of Museums, for a "big tent" uniting all American Museums; by Elaine Gurian, the conscience of museums; and by Al DeSena, the advancer of informal learning.

My deepest gratitude and love go to my partner in everything, Jeanie Stahl, for her guidance and support.

Preface

I love museums and want what's best for them because I believe museums are good for society. I've loved working in museums for decades while watching our field grow, evolve, and mature, but I think museums could be even better. Although recent years have been challenging, I have faith that we will get our act together, prove our lasting value, and help build a better and more democratic society.

Organizational psychologist Adam Grant, in his wise book *Think Again* (Viking, 2021), advised "let go of knowledge and opinions that are no longer serving you well. . . . A hallmark of wisdom is knowing when to abandon some of your most cherished tools." This book rethinks traditional museum practices to suggest updates that can make museums even more effective.

I write this book to you, assuming you are a fellow museum professional, also in love with museums and hungry to make museums more relevant, more inspiring, and more effective. I trust your heart to protect and enhance museums, leading them to evolve as their communities evolve, to develop strong character, and to lead by example.

Our minds have been busy generating a wealth of museum literature full of ideas, research findings, and principles. This book is based on this foundation. All my suggestions build on the work of insightful colleagues and fellow museum professionals.

My mind is currently at that wonderful age when it works to recall the past, yet no longer needs to work to earn its keep. My brain is full of museum observations over five decades of museum experience. I've learned lots of lessons that may save younger folks some time, but more usefully, I have recently had the time to make some sense of what I've learned and to sort all this input into suggestions for new and potentially more effective museum practices.

The museum field has given me so much that I value, and now I want to return that love. Call me a Dutch Uncle, though I'm Danish . . . well, also Australian . . . also Canadian . . . well, in the end, very American, as you will see.

It is a good time for museums to change: time to shed outdated practices and expectations and adapt innovations that take advantage of new opportunities. During the Museum Boom (1980s–2008), we focused on adding space; now is the time to focus on making existing museums more effective: more productive in more ways for more people for more impact and value and more social enterprise in our role as agents of positive social change. It is about investing, not in new buildings but in the infrastructure of the buildings we have and how we use them. It is time to redefine growth from visitor attendance and gallery square feet to engagements, occupancy, quality, impact, and value. We should not focus on more museums but on more effective museums.

"Effective (adj): Works well and produces the desired result." (Macmillan Dictionary .com)

We are needlessly hampered by archaic museum practices developed in response to past conditions tainted by patriarchal and racist biases. Museums are no longer expected to be fortresses, commanding authorities, elite clubhouses, patronized nonprofits, people magnets, and cash cows, yet many of our practices still reflect those agendas. It is heartening to see many museums shedding historic baggage. Museums have changed over the last decades. Proof that museums can change is evidenced by the survivors of the pandemic lockdowns. Museums are now valued for a wealth of beneficial results beyond their focused missions. Yet, the old baggage still weighs down museum practices of mission, staff organization, governance, operating revenues, programming, marketing and development, fiduciary responsibilities, and more. This book suggests new ways.

The aim of *The Effective Museum: Rethinking Museum Practices to Increase Impact* is to provide every museum professional with practical suggestions for how to be more successful at achieving a museum's intentional purposes. Specifically, I am writing for museum professionals who see themselves as agents of change, passionately driven to make their museums as effective as they can be, even if the evolution disrupts and challenges.

I hope that museum professionals will find all the suggestions interesting and worthy of consideration. Some of the suggestions may fit your museum but not others. Some suggestions may seem wonderful, but too much hassle to get through. For these good but difficult ideas, phasing and experimenting during the initial steps will help spread the effort as you start to see the benefits.

Although the suggestions are ambitious in potential impact, only a few increase costs (more increase revenue). The rest can be handled within normal operations, resulting in greater efficiency. For the most part, they are innovative ways to rethink traditional museum practices.

CRISES, TRENDS, AND CHANGES IN THE MUSEUM FIELD

The ideas in this book respond to the field's current trends—the growth of digital and other programming, the soul searching around racism, the need for diversity, equity, access, and inclusion (DEAI), and the heightened role expected of museums as identity and symbolic platforms, in addition to the pandemic impacts. The suggestions also reflect the major shifts due to previous crises over the decades—the shift from collections to education as a museum's primary purpose; the imperative to address both excellence and equity; the growth of earned revenue and its enablers, branding and marketing; universal access; gender equity; green museums; the participatory museum; repatriation; social media; the shift from missionary preaching to community service; from new bricks and mortar during the Museum Boom to no growth in the Great Recession—to name a few of the seismic shifts in the field from the 1970s to the 2010s before #MeToo, Black Lives Matter, and the pandemic hit.

In some respects, all museum books aspire to make museums more effective in some way, but this book focuses on rethinking the nuts and bolts of museum operations in response to these shifts and trends.

The suggestions are for postpandemic museums that are on their own journeys to new kinds of normal. In practice, museums never reach normal; we have always been in change, constantly struggling for sustainable stability while our communities' shifting needs create new opportunities and threats. Whether the suggestions seem incremental or disruptive, the aim is to help museums evolve to their full potential.

The Effective Museum might help you revise your museum's conceptual framework, revitalize your audiences and supporters, reorganize your museum, reinvest in your resources (staff, collections, facilities, etc.), reposition your programming, and restore management basics. This book seeks to help you rethink these key museum practices.

This book is intended for most, but not all, American museums. I am not trying to reach commercial museums, private collection museums, or corporate museums, but I care about all public museums, including nonprofit, university, government, and tribal museums in all the American Alliance of Museums' (AAM) list of museum sectors and disciplines.

Some of the suggestions are designed to make museums more effective by increasing volume/scale and efficiency of the museum's activities, rather than by advocating new ways of being effective. Museums already know how to be effective; these suggestions can help them be more effective by jettisoning outdated museum practices and serving more people more efficiently.

The Effective Museum will present a diversity of suggestions and not a single system. However, the suggestions share definitions and frameworks and a unifying voice and structure. While any museum can adopt whichever suggestions you want, the last chapter helps you explore how the suggestions might be mutually reinforcing.

SUMMARY OF THE SUGGESTIONS

Each chapter typically includes (1) generalized statement of a problem and the need for new ideas; (2) new suggestions implementable in many museums; (3) the likely resistance; (4) a summation of the idea's potential impacts and benefits; and (5) the start of an implementation process. To avoid repetitions, I stray from this structure toward the end. The suggestions vary in form—some are suggested strategies and others are lists of options or research questions or implementation steps. The last suggestion is just a short sentence, but the pages of museum history that lead up to it provide the rationale.

The book's suggestions are organized into seven parts, each reflecting a different aspect of museum practice. As your museum may be interested in some but not all these suggestions, the following summary is offered to help you chose what to read first:

Part I Revise Your Conceptual Framework

Chapter 1 Pluralize Missions and Elevate Values: Serve multiple revenue sources within your guiding principles.

Part II Revitalize Your Audiences and Supporters

Chapter 2 Redefine the Relationship between Philanthropy and Governance: Rethink governance structures to reduce conflicts of interest, provide supporters the benefits they desire, spread the workload, and clarify roles.

Chapter 3 Recognize the Competitive Marketplace for Your Revenues: All revenue must be fought for and won; your museum can compete better by integrating your sales forces and strategies.

Chapter 4 Serve your Community, Audiences, and Supporters: Determine if your museum's culture aligns with your business model.

Part III Reorganize Your Museum

Chapter 5 Move from We/Them to Us/Us: Guide museum programming and policy by representatives of the audiences you wish to serve.

Chapter 6 Reorganize the Museum as a Producing Organization: Regroup your resources to produce programs for all physical and virtual spaces.

Chapter 7 Unify the Museum Field: Work with other museums to share more through five intermural and field-wide suggestions.

Part IV Reinvest in Your Resources

Chapter 8 Invest in Infrastructure, Not New Structure: Increase the use, flexibility, and productivity of your existing spaces.

Chapter 9 Leverage Existing Assets: Discover and monetize your museum's unrealized and unexplored capital resources.

Part V Reposition Your Programming

Chapter 10 Select Your Creative Talents Effectively: Adjust to contracting practices used by other creative industries such as theater, movies, and publishing.

Chapter 11 Support New Strategies for Changing Programming: It needs to cost less to stay fresh; work with other museums to reduce costs per user while increasing shared quality.

Part VI Restore Management Basics

Chapter 12 Measure, Document, and Communicate Your Impacts: Use data strategically to prove and improve your impact and effectiveness.

Chapter 13 Get Real about Financials: Move toward compliance with normal fiscal and accounting practices for stability and resilience.

Chapter 14 Plan your Future: Know your response options for unknown crises, yet incubate promising innovations.

Part VII Reimagine Museum Models

Chapter 15 Embrace Public Mandates: Serving your audiences and supporters is important but not as important as serving society.

Chapter 16 Integrate the Suggestions: Imagine the Effective Museum and the Programmable Museum

In chapter 16, I summarize each chapter's potential impact in one paragraph.

DEFINITIONS AND FRAMEWORKS

I use terms and definitions based on familiar museum practice but applied more broadly. An important example: I use the term *museum engagements* to collect attendance at all the museum's activities—gallery attendance, lecture series attendance, volunteer shifts, board meetings, interactions with partners, outreach participations, etc.—into one number. A *physical museum engagement* is defined as one person-trip to a museum site or to a museum-sponsored program off-site by a person not employed or contracted by the museum to be there. The *person-trip* is a measure of effort spent by the person (time and often money are also spent). *Virtual museum engagements* involve much less effort by the participant, but still require time.

I use *community* and *your community* as convenient shorthand for the pool of possible constituents and stakeholders that a museum serves, also called the *market*, the *customer base*, the *public and civic sphere*, and the *region*. I recognize that this simplification can hide the complexities of all the communities a museum may choose to serve plus those who think the museum should be serving them. As you read, you should replace *community* with your own term for the collected people and organizations you serve.

Yet, museums are not engineered entities with precise edges, and some definitions have fuzzy borders. Museums are organic, fluid, and changing. Many lofty terms like *value, impact, performance*, and *benefit* elude precise definitions and measurements. Many terms are roughly synonymous but with different baggage. A particularly freighted group of synonyms includes *ends, purposes, missions, goals, outcomes, perceived benefits, impacts, returns on investments*, and *values*. A museum may want all these to result from its activities, but each term carries somewhat different expectations, resulting in confusion that impedes collaboration and improvement.

I want to be as clear as possible, so my terms and their definitions are used consistently in all chapters, although I recognize each museum has its own nuanced version of such terms as *visitor* and *outreach*. Because the lack of shared language and definitions is one of the museum field's main obstacles, I have taken care to base my terms on the field's most tested and accepted definitions where available. These definitions are best when specific, like *site visitor*, but we also need more inclusive terms, like *program participants* and *virtual visitors*, and largely unmeasured terms, like *dwell time*.

As used in this book, *impact* and *benefit* are both words for the outcomes of a museum's activities. They may describe the same outcome but recognize a difference in perspective: Impacts are what the museum wants to accomplish; benefits are what the community, audiences, and supporters want from the museum. Because this book is written to help museum professionals improve impact, that word is emphasized in preference.

THE MUSEUM THEORY OF ACTION

The Museum Theory of Action assumes a museum produces its impacts and benefits through iterations of a sequence of logic model–like steps as described in the following constructed narrative: (1) Museum leadership (or other forces), in response to perceived community needs and aspirations, determine the museum's *intentional purposes*; (2) leadership and staff filter the many possibilities for achieving those purposes by the museum's *guiding principles* to select the museum's *desired impacts* and their intended *audiences* and *supporters*; (3) staff, with their knowledge of the museum's *resources*, produce (e.g., plan, design, test, fabricate/create, market, deliver and operate); (4) the museum's *activities*, using a constantly iterative cycle of; (5) evaluation

Table 0.1.   Museum Theory of Action: From Intentional Purposes to Perceived Benefits

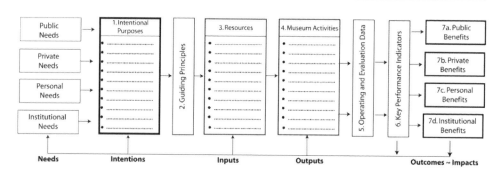

and operating data that feed into; (6) the museum's *key performance indicators* that monitor; (7) the *impacts* and *benefits* the museum is providing its audiences and funders, which feed back to the beginning as one source of their perceived *community needs* and aspirations (see table 0.1).

You can adapt the Museum Theory of Action as a template for narrating how your museum will achieve its purposes.[1]

Each of the chapters add concepts and language to this preface, and every defined term appears in the index. The chapters start with a museum's ideology, consider its stakeholders' interests, suggest reorganizations of museum operations, rethink resources and programming, recommit to management principles, and conclude with evolving and reimagining museums.

The shared goal of all my suggestions is to help you make your museum more effective at achieving your purposes.

WHY I HAVE WRITTEN THIS BOOK NOW

Each of these chapters could be a book, but neither of us has the time for that bookshelf. Each chapter describes a handful of related suggestions at a big-picture level—just a sketch, in truth. My goal is to start conversations, not to blueprint conversions. These suggestions can't be implemented without your efforts to adapt one or more of the suggestions to your museum's situation.

Before the pandemic lockdowns, it was hard to implement big changes because of entrenched operating policies and revenue expectations. Now, suggestions are both needed and possible.

I look at museums as social and economic operations. As a museum planner, I needed to take the long, integrated view in the master plans we created for our museum clients. Through experience with many museums over many decades, I observed the rich diversity of museums, and I see our shared patterns of professional practice that link a wonderfully varied collection of museums. All museums I respect seek to "change lives," but each museum has its own goals, resources, activities, audiences, supporters, and impacts.

In attitude, *The Effective Museum* is not *thou shall*, but much more *think about trying this suggestion*. In style, *The Effective Museum* aims to be inspiring, reflective, fun to read, and useful.

The tone of this book is intentionally personal, friendly, reflective, and narrative. It is as light as I can make a book about abstract operational tactics. You know your museum's context and I don't; I hope you will take these suggestions further by translating my generalized suggestions into the reality of your museum.

Underlying all my suggestions is a new way of thinking about museums, based on assumptions about how they can be more effective at achieving their purposes. This language, drawn from museum use and defined in textboxes, reflects Adam Grant's "rethinking" in the opening quote.

In short, this book is my legacy to the field and is based on my experiences. This is my attempt to help you by sharing what I've learned. With more than five decades of museum work, I suggest rethinking museum practices as a basis for you to build your own learning and legacy.

NOTE

1. For a complete description and rationale for the Museum Theory of Action, see my book *Measuring Museum Impact and Performance*, chapter 1 (Rowman & Littlefield, 2016).

Part I
REVISE YOUR CONCEPTUAL FRAMEWORK

These first suggestions are not about rewriting your mission statement . . . again. They are about revising the roles that mission, vision, values, stakeholders, and business model might play in defining, prioritizing, and increasing your desired impacts.

1

Pluralize Missions and Elevate Values

If you have worked in a museum for a few years, you have probably sat in on a visioning workshop, perhaps many: A wall full of stickies and a couple of flip charts face a clutter of chairs. All the stickies with blue dots are now in the center, and the green ones and the purples are on the left. The wall on the right is ominously empty, blocked by a trestle table with leftover sandwiches and a tub of wet soda cans. Over lunch, everyone put gold stars on the stickies they thought were best. The facilitator drags the table aside, sticks up all the gold stars, stares at them awhile, shuffles their order once or twice, and pronounces, "There, that's the basis for your mission statement!"

My experience is that many mission statements come to agreement out of a combination of safe choices and exhaustion. Safe choices are typically lofty public-spirited educational goals, and exhaustion is, well, when everybody has said everything they want to say several times. The mission statements that come out of such processes rarely address the other contributions the museum provides.

Despite the reverence paid to them, mission statements seldom last forever. New directors tend to launch a new strategic plan, which entails revising the mission statement and developing a set of goals and objectives along with a grand, even epic, vision statement. The more people this process involves, the better it is for buy-in.

Museum missions often change over time. At a more granular level, I've noticed that many museums pursue a series of more defined purposes, which change even more rapidly in response to our changing community needs.

If our mission statement—formerly a museum's foundational rock—changes, how is a museum to anchor its conceptual framework? What is constant?

The museum's values. Values are relatively stable—they change but slower than purposes. Although your missions and intentional purposes should evolve to stay in tune with your community's needs, your values are who you are.

What's a museum professional to do? This chapter suggests ways to revise your conceptual framework.

A museum's *conceptual framework* (i.e., core ideology) is the theoretical foundation for everything it does. I am suggesting that a museum's conceptual framework might have five main parts: intentional purposes, guiding principles, vision, stakeholders, and business model.

- *Purposes* are about why a museum does what it does.
- *Guiding principles* are about how a museum does what it does.
- *Vision* is the big picture goal.
- *Stakeholders* are who the museum impacts or benefits.
- *Business model* is the mixture of value propositions that sustains and grows the museum's services to its stakeholders.

Table 1.1 summarizes these suggested changes in language and use.

Why make these changes? To adapt to the museum's reality of multiple customer categories, to relate the parts to each other in a clear theory of action, and to set up the museum to measure and increase its desired impacts, traceable to its intentional purposes.

This chapter addresses how to accommodate multiple customers and to elevate the museum's guiding principles to the prominence previously accorded to mission. Chapter 3 looks at business models, and chapter 4 addresses community and stakeholders. Chapter 12 shows how to use these relationships to measure and increase impact.

Table 1.1.   Conceptual Framework: Suggested Language Changes

Traditional Language	Suggested New Language
Core and Strategic Values	Guiding Principles
Mission Statement	Intentional Purpose 1
	Intentional Purpose 2
Objectives, Goals, and Strategies	Intentional Purpose 3
	Intentional Purpose 4
Impacts and Outcomes	Desired Impacts and Perceived Benefits
Vision Statement	Vision Statement
Market	Community
Visitors, Users, Guests, and Customers	Audiences: Visitors and Program Participants
Donors, Funders, Sponsors, Partners, Collectors, and Volunteers	Supporters: Public and Private
Value Proposition; Business Model	Business Model

REASONS TO CHANGE

Once conceptual frameworks were done, I seldom found that staff—much less contractors and architects—knew how to apply them. If the mission statement was sharply focused, it discouraged other ways the museum could be beneficial. But if it was too broadly written, then everything was possible. How do you use the mission statement to think about staff unionization, for instance?

Museums are complicated, diverse, and serve their communities in many ways not reflected in focused mission statements. In the last five decades museums have gone way beyond just offering several exhibit galleries to a number of visitors. We are alive with programs, we reach out beyond our walls, and we engage audiences and supporters in many activities, including our visitor experiences. Simplicity, especially in focused mission statements, is neither an accurate nor a useful approach to American public museums. We've grown complicated.

The current reality is that many US museums already operate as community service museums and pursue multiple purposes, which results in multiple kinds of outcomes. They provide corporations with visibility and connections; they provide visitors with quality family experiences; and they provide cities with identity and add to the cultural infrastructure. They are community gathering places and resources for K–12 educators. Such museums are constantly changing their mix in response to the interests and needs of their audiences and supporters.

This is good, and the museum community should not feel guilty about it, but listen harder to the operating data, and then look creatively for the common ground between the museum's intentions and its audiences' and supporters' intentions. Museums can track their changing value through operating numbers and observe the shifting ratios to inform planning and to keep the museum responsive to its external community.

For instance, a zoo's mission might be wildlife conservation, but families value it for outings, employers for its quality-of-life contributions, economic development agencies for its jobs and tourism impacts, and corporations for its community relations benefits. Learning is one of a visitor's values, but it is often secondary to other personal values such as using the museum for quality leisure time with friends and family.

These are all valid and beneficial community values and not inherently in conflict with wildlife conservation. They also show up among the zoo's annual revenues as admissions, memberships, public funds, and corporate sponsorships. There is nothing wrong with the public valuing a museum for some benefit it provides outside its mission purpose. Further, the public will likely get even better value if the museum becomes purposeful and intentional about providing that benefit.

Yet, all these museums swore by their mission. They believed that their mission should inform everything that they do and that everything else was there simply to enable them to pursue their focused mission. One museum instituted a caste system dividing mission-central staff from mission-enabling activities, granting educators more importance than function rental and theater operators. I observed, however, that whenever the so-called ancillary revenues were threatened, management still spent money and time to fix the issue.

Mission funding still exists for some message-driven museums, including corporate, government, and university museums as well as museums mostly funded to communicate their funders' content, such as the Koshland Science Museum (DC) and the Bullock Texas State History Museum (Austin). For those museums funded by funders with the same, single purpose, you can stick to one mission and skip this chapter.

However, most of America's large urban museums have adopted multiple customers (i.e., multiple revenue sources). To serve them more effectively, I suggest adopting multiple missions, which I redefine as *intentional purposes*.

PURSUE MULTIPLE PURPOSES FOR MULTIPLE REVENUES FOR GREATER SERVICE

The first suggestion is to become intentional about your multiple purposes. This requires unlearning the opinion that a single, focused mission should guide everything a museum does. Instead, learn from all the purposes you are currently achieving, and revise your conceptual framework to accommodate a prioritized list of your main community services.

Intentional purposes can be more specific than umbrella mission statements. This means they are more measurable because they define what outcomes your museum is trying to achieve.

Once an intentional purpose is stated, its desired outcomes should also be expressed. If we want to improve the world in some way, how will we know we have succeeded? What will be different? What will indicate that difference? If we are trying to grow social capital, for instance, the number of partnerships we support every year might be a good indicator of our success.

By establishing a small number of prioritized intentional purposes, the museum clarifies the main services it intends to offer, honors them with attention, and increases the quality and impact of each service, rather than focusing on just the mission-central services. Leadership can then establish departmental objectives and tie them to the annual budget and master plan. Management can ask those responsible for the museum's activities to articulate their theories of action about how their programs will achieve the desired impacts and benefits. Yearly tabulations of the number of engagements, support and earned revenues, and other evaluation factors can help leadership reward achievement, identify best practices, and increase overall impact.

VALUE YOUR VALUES OVER YOUR MISSIONS

My second suggestion is to enshrine your values on the altar formerly occupied by your mission. But be gentle, and do it over time. Mission has been dominant for a long time and retains a loyal following.

Traditionally, museums have emblazoned their mission statements in their lobby, on the back of business cards, even on needlepoint samplers. In some museums, every employee is expected to memorize it.

My suggestion is to treat your values that way instead. Values are who you are. They are your character, your reputation, and your brand identity. Put them everywhere, and encourage staff and contractors to live by them and to make decisions by them.

Because the word *value* has so many different meanings, and because I want to use *value* economically, as in, "What is the value of a museum engagement to a visitor," I prefer using *guiding principles* for what many others call corporate or cultural values.

Well-run museums already operate by their guiding principles. Museums care about accuracy and truth. Museums respect their visitors and their community. Increasingly, museums strive to be diverse and to represent all voices in decision-making. Museums care about quality and setting an example. Museums strive for excellence and equity.

Science museums value the processes of science. Art museums value our visual culture, history museums value history, and children's museums value child development. In this way, the museum's disciplinary choice, often made decades ago, can become one of its guiding principles, as well as appear among the intentional purposes.

Your guiding principles are also your museum's protection from exploitation. You have your museum's honor and reputation to protect. Community needs can come from all sectors, some with considerable pressure on the museum and some with conflicts of interest. How does a museum avoid supporting a corrupt politician? Hosting a KKK reunion? Partnering with an exploiter? A firmly held set of guiding principles can anchor a museum and serve as a decision filter: Is this idea consistent with our guiding principles? Does it reflect our character and enhance our reputation?

POTENTIAL RESISTANCE

I realize I am suggesting a significant reshuffling of the traditional order and that implementing these suggestions is likely to meet the kinds of resistance I describe in this section.

The concept of mission is deeply ingrained in museum culture and is closely tied to the idea that museums exist for the public good. The American Alliance of Museums' (AAM) *National Standards & Best Practices* for US museums includes an evaluation standard establishing the primacy of mission: "All aspects of the museum's operations are integrated and focused on meeting its mission."

The problem for museums, however, is that most midsize to large museums do not have the luxury of focused missions because they also must serve the diverse missions of their paying audiences and supporters. They provide multiple public goods.

Guiding principles are distinct from intentional purposes. Purposes define what outcomes you are after, while your guiding principles influence how you pursue those outcomes. Hence, resistance may come from those who want the accountability from the museum's conceptual framework that mission supposedly provided. With my suggestions, accountability will be clearer from your prioritized intentional purposes, and you can evaluate whether the activities meet the standards of your guiding principles.

Your list of guiding principles is likely to be inherently fuzzy, nonmeasurable, and nonprioritized. You can't say that excellence is more important than respect, nor can you easily measure respect, for instance.

There are bound to be staff and external critics who will challenge the museum for not following its own guiding principles, using them against the museum in arguing their case. These may be justified criticisms, if made constructively. The museum should always question whether its activities are true to its guiding principles.

INCREASED IMPACTS AND BENEFITS

To increase impact, and to measure that increase, a museum should first define the impact it desires and then figure out what data fields might measure success at achieving that impact.

Museum colleagues and I tested this approach to measuring a museum's impact with six participating New England museums. We called this the *PIID Sequence*: For each of your *purposes*, define your desired *impacts* (what will be better?). Then, what might *indicate* that impact is happening (what change might we observe?) and what *data fields* can measure that indicator (how do we measure that change?). See chapter 12 for more about the PIID Sequence.

Replacing a blanket mission statement with several prioritized and more specific intentional purposes is fundamental to measuring and, therefore, improving impact. If you wish, you might adapt your old mission as your top priority purpose.

A prioritized list of intentional purposes also makes your museum more accountable. It facilitates planning by providing realistic ranges for future performance objectives. It makes museum leadership clear by acknowledging multiple priorities, and it gets rid of the class distinction between mission and nonmission activities.

When a museum's conceptual framework is founded on its guiding principles, everything it does should reflect those guiding principles. This foundation is more comprehensive than a changing mission statement that doesn't cover everything the museum does. More importantly, your guiding principles are who you are. To follow them is to be true to yourself. Collectively, your guiding principles are your museum's definition of *museum quality*.

Basing program development, staff training, publications, and social media on the museum's guiding principles will coordinate everything the museum produces. The growth of museum branding suggests that communicating institutional character and enforcing brand identity and product consistency have helped museums.

STEPS TO ADAPT THE IDEAS TO YOUR MUSEUM

The first step to implement any of these suggestions is to *socialize* the idea among your colleagues. I learned the term in Canada, where it is common to introduce new ideas in a series of conversations with stakeholders. Socializing an idea does not move it forward, but it does give you a sense of how it will be received and how it might work in your organization.

The second step, which also applies to most suggestions, is to research the museum's history of mission statements and lists of objectives and key strategies. What other kinds of purposes has the museum pursued?

Analyze the museum's annual exchange tallies to identify your largest services. Of your museum's annual engagements, how many of them are for your visitor experience, your online programs, your outreach, your volunteers, etc.? Of your annual operating revenues, what shares are from visitors, scheduled program participants, and private and public supporters? This research will help define who is getting the most value from their benefits from the museum. Once the research is complete, assess at a policy level whether the museum's leadership is content with the current status or has aspirations to shift the balances.

Expand your research to peer museums to find out what purposes they are providing their stakeholders. Talk to local leadership about community needs your museum might support.

Lastly, look at the list of categories of potential museum impact and benefit (table 12.1) to see which ones you are already serving or might expand.

Then your leadership team can begin to list, clump, shortlist, wordsmith, and eventually prioritize a manageable number of three to five intentional purposes and their desired impacts and benefits. See the list of purposes in table 1.2.

I am suggesting that your museum might look at your current values, consider relabeling them as guiding principles, and make them the foundation and main credo of your conceptual framework.

Of course, first you might make sure that the list reflects what the museum believes now. Maybe it includes what you aspire to become. Tables 1.3 and 1.4 provide a checklist of some of the core and strategic values held by museums I've worked with. Are some of these better descriptors for your museum's current and aspirational character?

Table 1.2. Example: Prioritized Intentional Purposes

Intentional Purpose 1 (old mission statement): Spark interest and engagement in creativity and innovation and their impact—past, present, future—on our city and our lives.
Desired Impact (DI) 1.1: Audiences report increased interest.
DI 1.2: Teachers report increased student engagement.

Intentional Purpose 2: Contribute public value to the community.
DI 2.1: Regional residents claim the museum adds to their quality of life.
DI 2.2: More residents attend our free festivals.
DI 2.3: Residents are proud to live here.

Intentional Purpose 3: Help build local economic value.
DI 3.1: Neighbors believe the museum adds to their home value.
DI 3.2: Local payroll and purchasing increase.
DI 3.3: Engagements with our career programs increase.
DI 3.4: Our share of nonresident (tourist) audiences remains constant or grows.

Table 1.3. Partial Checklist of Guiding Principles: Short

Accessibility	Disciplined	Honoring diversity
Accuracy	Diversity	Innovation
Art	Education	Learning
Authenticity	Engaging	Nature
Boldness	Entrepreneurship	Partnerships
Cleanliness	Everyone	Passionate
Community identity	Excellence	Preservation
Connection	Fiscal, ethical & legal responsibility	Quality
Creative	Freedom	Respect
Cross-cultural exchanges	Fun	Scholarship
Current and relevant	Fun visitor experiences	Science
Customer-focused	History	Service
Defining the region		Thoughtful

Table 1.4. Partial Checklist of Guiding Principles: Phrases

The museum is responsive to the community.
The museum is popular and visitor focused.
The museum nurtures a strong sense of place.
The museum is a forum for public dialogue.
The museum is a forefront institution run on sound economics.
The museum is a community collaborator.
The museum is a catalyst for social change.
The museum bases its programs on scholarship and collections.
The museum is a public learning resource.
The museum is community oriented.
The museum is a delta institution built for change.

You may find that your museum deeply believes in some guiding principles that you have not expressed, such as fiscal responsibility and teamwork. Some museums distinguish between core values (forever true) and strategic values (aspirational). This is your opportunity to expand your list of guiding principles to reflect the character traits most important to your museum.

Some of your guiding principles can be umbrellas embracing a larger family of related principles. For instance, respect for others can include safety, kindness, welcoming, diversity, openness, and transparency. Because transparency, for instance, is not obviously related to respect, these linkages and families of kindred principles should be discussed among staff on a regular basis—much the way mission used to be discussed regularly.

Once you have confirmed your list of guiding principles, use them as another set of filters. As an idea moves through internal discussion, check in with your list of guiding principles to help winnow out incompatible ideas while shaping the idea to better reflect the museum's brand identity. Is the idea accurate? Is the idea respectful of others? Is the idea affordable and prudent? Is the idea engaging and fun? In the next chapter, I outline a review panel that could refine proposed ideas to better fit within the guiding principles.

I suggest you make your guiding principles as visible as your mission used to be. Encourage all who work for the museum to take pride in doing museum-quality work and to know what achieving that quality entails.

It is time to develop a conceptual framework that meets the reality of American museums as unique organizations with unique business models serving their communities in multiple ways and guided by their principles.

Part II
REVITALIZE YOUR AUDIENCES AND SUPPORTERS

They are who you are serving. Yes, museums exist for their communities, but your museum's actual engagements are with those individuals and funders within the community who choose to engage with the museum. Because they have a choice, you must court them. What do they want? What benefits are they seeking from their museum engagements?

Redefine the Relationship between Philanthropy and Governance

I believe that one of the oldest legacies from the patriarchal museums of the mid-twentieth century is the presumption that the museum's wealthy supporters should also govern it as trustees and board members. Recently, headline cases of compromised donors, such as the Sacklers and Jeffrey Epstein, have sullied the museums and universities involved. The Whitney Museum faced a conflict between a board member's armament company and an artwork critical of its product's impact on its victims. Social media, identity politics, and a widening income gap amplify these issues.

In addition to explicit decisions, both good and bad, museums can be faulted for decisions they did not make, also known as sins of omission. Recently, museums have been blamed for ill-gotten collections, patriarchal biases, gender inequality, insensitivity to race and culture, and conflicts of interest, none of which were explicit decisions, but rather unquestioned legacies from previous times. These are particularly difficult issues for volunteer board members who have enough trouble getting up to speed on the decisions at hand.

If the museum is successful at qualifying for directors and officers (D&O) insurance, a good policy can protect board members from personal financial liability for the museum's issues; however, there is still social culpability, erosion of reputation, and a sense of failure that no insurance covers.

It is no longer desirable to assume the very rich should determine policy, yet almost all museums depend on contributed income. The current situation is fraught with potential conflicts and unreasonable demands and expectations. Yet museums are not about to turn their backs on their supporters and backers. This chapter explores how we might improve the situation.

THE PURPOSE OF FINDING A SOLUTION

What solutions might we explore that will retain our philanthropists while democratizing governance and reducing conflicts of interest? While we are at it, another question gets at the fundamentals: Who should determine the museum's conceptual framework, particularly its selection of intentional purposes, guiding principles, intended audiences, and business models? Who accepts fiduciary responsibility for the museum? Who governs the museum? Who's responsible for it?

The objective of rethinking a museum's governance structure might be to design a system linking a few entities with a division of responsibilities that collectively steers the museum toward ever more effective services to its communities while reducing conflicts and sharing the workloads.

I'll wrap all these issues into the term *governance*. A museum's governors are responsible for the museum. Although there are other terms, I will call the official collection of governors, directors, or trustees the museum's *board.*

Governance, however, is a formal term. In practice, a museum's actual *power structure* and its *chain of command* may be different.

Most formal chains of command show the museum's CEO reporting to the board, and all other staff reporting upward through a hierarchical organization chart to the CEO.

Others besides board members can exert significant influence on a museum's policy choices. Partners that provide some revenue, such as the school system, local corporations, supporting foundations, and community agencies, have clear influence as prime customers. Representatives of organizations who seek to influence the museum but do not provide direct revenue include the media (both press and social media), special interest groups, peer museums, government departments, and cultural agencies.

SCOPE OF GOVERNANCE: COLLECTED BOARD EXPECTATIONS

I started by considering the many expectations that museums have for their boards of directors. Those expectations include ethics, responsibilities, and specific tasks, which together I'll call the *scope of governance.*

Among those are items that conflict with others, such as the expectation for wealth and the edict against conflicts of interest. Today, board members with significant wealth are likely to have conflicts of interest between the museum's interests and some of their holdings or their allegiances to other boards.

Governance has *fiduciary responsibility* for the museum. There must be some publicly accountable and legally responsible entity that manages the museum's assets and makes sure that funds are used as the funding sources stipulated. Fiduciary responsibility includes working solely in the museum's best interests, forbidding conflicts of interest, and obeying all applicable rules and policies. Ignorance of any of these issues does not forgive liability.

Nonprofit board members are legally and ethically bound by common law to at least these three duties:

1. The duty of care: Members must actively engage with board meetings, materials, and activities; know how to read financial reports and management analysis; and use at least the same care as any prudent and ordinary person would.
2. The duty of loyalty: Members must put the interest of the museum ahead of any other interest, including their own. Members must disclose conflicts of interest and not use the position for personal or commercial gain.
3. The duty of obedience: Members must make sure the museum obeys the law and does nothing illegal. Members must carry out the museum's purposes using its guiding principles.

In addition to these formal duties, some rules of thumb set up expectations for board members, and it may be time to question these:

- The Three Ts (Time, Treasure, and Talent) assume board members give their time freely to the museum, have treasure to contribute generously, and offer their talents to the museum's use.
- Noses In, Fingers Out (NIFO) assumes board members should observe staff operations from time to time but not interfere directly with staff or their decisions.

Traditional boards carry heavy fundraising expectations, sometimes including minimum annual donations from all board members plus active solicitations from their friends and associates. Some museums use metrics such as the percentage of board members contributing, the average contribution, and comparisons to goals to shame the members into meeting their quotas.

Further, when the museum runs a deficit and depletes its cash reserves, board members are often expected to make up the deficit.

No wonder boards are populated with the wealthy.

The Carver Model of Policy Governance teaches that the governing board should determine policy and that professional staff should decide on appropriate strategies to execute that policy. This provides a clear distinction, but one that is often ignored.

Governance includes setting policy by evolving the museum's *conceptual framework* (see chapter 1) as well as approving key operating policies, such as the museum's collection policy and human resources policy.

Programming selection is particularly sensitive. If governance is properly divided between the board and staff, then the board's role is to determine programming policy but leave the actual choices of content to staff. Programming *policy* might include guidance as to style, learning philosophy, target audiences, desired outcomes, and other top-level issues. Programming *strategy* and *tactics* are the appropriate domain of staff professionals, including choices of exhibitions, lectures, programs, website, and social media activity. Staff decide on the museum's programming following guidance provided by governance.

Nevertheless, special interest groups can put pressure on board members to direct staff to remove or change exhibit and program content. This creates awkward situations, especially if the public believes board members have the authority to dictate any decision.

In addition to setting policy, the board needs to review and approve the museum's annual budget, major restricted donations, significant collection additions, as well as capital project budgets, logo changes, and other major decisions. Board members are also tasked to make judgments, advocate for the museum, monitor and evaluate the museum's performance, conduct periodic audits, develop the board, learn about museums, and hire and fire the CEO.

In short, the list of tasks and duties for board members is long, scary, and mined with potential conflicts. Considering these issues, unbundling the tasks and separating the conflicts into a few distinct entities with defined scopes and relationships makes sense to me, and might apply to your museum.

SUGGESTIONS THAT COULD INCREASE IMPACT

My suggestions explore models for separating policy governance from philanthropy. The idea is to hold onto to donors by offering them the benefits they desire in return for their donations and to delegate some aspects of the scope of governance to other entities.

Military service museums, as well as many other government- and university-owned museums, have a governance model that might be adapted by more independent museums. Because government employees are not allowed to solicit or accept money or engage in advocacy, their museums form foundations to raise money and run revenue-generating activities. In these instances, there are two entities, one officially in change with members appointed largely by the owner and the other a nonprofit foundation with a self-perpetuating membership composed of people of means and access to resources.

It may make sense to separate the financial oversight of operating budgets from capital budgets. The board of directors would approve operating budgets and the foundation would approve capital budgets because they are the ones to raise that money. I suggest establishing a protocol for the board to generate proposals for capital projects for which the foundation is to raise money. The museum's operations, funded by its operating revenues, is a regular activity of the museum and should be overseen by the board. However, the foundation might have some oversight on how capital funds are spent to ensure compliance with donor stipulations.

This suggestion contemplates several entities, each with specific duties and relationships to each other and the rest of the museum. Your museum is likely to have one or more of them already, probably using other names and with other ways of sorting out the scopes of governance. Your museum also has specific needs that will further shape the suggestion:

- Board of Directors: Responsible for the museum.
  - Fiduciary responsibility
  - Liability for the museum
  - Executive committee (chair + some committee chairs)
  - Conceptual framework (vision, purposes, etc.)
  - Compliance with the law
  - Management oversight
  - Hire/fire CEO
  - Standing and ad hoc committees
  - Policy development and approval
  - Operating approvals
  - Capital project proposals to the foundation

- Foundation: Responsible for raising funds and overseeing whether those funds are spent as stipulated (reports to the board).
  - Raise operating support and capital funds
  - Executive committee representative (voting member)
  - Capital project committee
  - Fundraising committee
  - Approve capital project proposals
  - Compliance with donor stipulations
  - Capital budget approvals
  - Represents the museum's supporters

- Community Access Forum: Responsible for soliciting and receiving outside input, acting as an open forum for special interest groups to express their desires. Staff reviews input and forwards to the review panel (reports to staff).
  - Executive committee representative (nonvoting member)
  - Community input (needs, special interest groups, etc.)
  - Advocacy and public relations
  - Represents the museum's communities and audiences

- Review Panel: Responsible for judging whether proposed ideas from any source serve the museum's intentional purposes and adhere to the guiding principles. Works directly with staff, may include staff, and should have the ability to send up red flags (reports to CEO).
  - Executive committee (nonvoting member)
  - Compliance with conceptual framework
  - May be the research and evaluation office

- CEO and Staff: Responsible for the strategies used to produce and operate the museum's activities and to develop its resources (CEO reports to the board).
  - Executive committee (CEO a nonvoting member)

Your museum can decide how many of these you want, who should be on them, whether paid or voluntary, their internal leadership, meeting frequency, and other bylaw and charter details. What is important is that the separation of powers puts arm's lengths between potential conflicts of interest, lessens the burden on volunteers, and focuses the scopes.

You can also decide who should people each entity. Ideally, members should have skills and resources that align with the scope for each. Further, members of each entity should reflect those they represent, as discussed in chapter 5.

By moving philanthropy from the board to the foundation, you free board members from fundraising, which allows for a more representative board that includes people who are not wealthy. Except in times of trouble, such board members would not be expected to donate or raise money, and might even be paid for meetings, as do some Canadian museums.

Most museums serve three sectors: their audiences, their supporters, and their community. Audiences include their visitors, program participants, and even nonusers who are aware of the museum and its programming. Supporters include donors, sponsors, foundations, and others who provide the museums capital and operating support funds. The museum also serves the community at large as an option to visit, regional symbol, local landmark, and an addition to the region's cultural and educational infrastructure.

My suggested division allows three of the entities to represent each of these sectors. The board, the final authority on the museum, can now focus on the audience, the museum's most important service sector. The foundation can focus on the supporters, building relationships with those who provide the museum's support funding, and the community input forum can focus on the community and its special interest groups.

POTENTIAL RESISTANCE

Inertia and bureaucracy are the two most likely obstructions to implementing these suggestions. Changes in governance often require changes in the bylaws and sometimes in the corporate charter. They also require careful hand-holding of the museum's key stakeholders, who may be leery of change.

The transition from your current governance structure to the future structure may be a difficult period with uncertain transition issues. Clarity around the benefits from making the change might motivate the efforts needed.

Donors and other stakeholders may worry about the loss of power and may reduce their commitment levels. Donors who may have felt full commitment as backers of the museum in its times of trouble may no longer feel as vested in the health of their museum. Empathetic donor stewardship can ease the transition.

Whenever a comprehensive responsibility assignment is divided into two or more parties, there is a danger that some tasks may not be covered, whereas others are doubly covered, causing confusion. Explicit division of responsibility into written scopes, coupled with a process for resolving confusion and conflicts, is essential to avoiding this.

Many museums that have foundations as well as boards of directors end up creating class distinctions between foundation activities and museum activities. When foundations develop staff, typically development and earned revenue specialists, tensions can arise between more highly paid foundation staff and sometimes civil service museum staff.

The foundation may get out in front of the board, raising funds for its own projects rather than carrying out the board-developed capital project proposals. Sometimes the foundation is separately incorporated, which means it has the right to refuse proposals. Some foundations use some of the funds they raise to pay their own staff, setting up potential conflicts or tensions with the museum's staff and board.

Managing multiple entities is likely to increase the CEO's workload and give the board chair more to coordinate to keep all entities unified in purposes and guiding principles. Clear protocols and staff assignments help, and another potential solution lies in being able to hand off other parts of their workload to the larger number of people involved.

These suggestions will be harder for smaller museums to implement when a small number of people must play multiple roles. In such instances, a plan to get there in the long term might keep current participants more aware of the potential interim issues.

INCREASED IMPACTS AND BENEFITS

The division of responsibilities that were formerly centralized in a board of directors into the suggested four entities spreads the tasks among more people, which should increase responsiveness, especially given limited volunteer time. By clarifying the principal responsibilities for each of the separate entities, those tasks will get more focused attention, resulting in greater effectiveness.

Engaging more volunteers strengthens the museum's connections to its community and makes it more responsive to community needs, increasing its effectiveness. More people meeting regularly on the museum's business will also increase the museum's engagement counts (see chapter 12).

Conflicts of interest, which introduce factors benefiting parties other than the museum, are inherently factors that reduce the museum's effectiveness. Therefore, reducing conflicts of interest should increase the museum's effectiveness.

Establishing a foundation whose primary function is fundraising and the oversight of how those funds are spent may increase the amount of support funding available to the museum.

STEPS TO ADAPT THE IDEAS TO YOUR MUSEUM

Because types of governance vary among museums, the museum needs to start this process by being clear about its current power structure and whether it is ready to shift to a more formal governance structure.

Is the museum's current power structure fair and honest? Does it reflect the museum's guiding principles and serve its intentional purposes? Is it accessible to stakeholders, including staff? Might these suggestions help you evolve a better governance structure?

3

Recognize the Competitive Marketplace for Your Revenues

I have found museums get queasy when talking about money. Some see raising funds as begging and hosting crowd-pleasers as selling out. Boasting about revenues, they fear, may inspire competitors or tax collectors and can be as gauche as bragging about one's salary. A museum's finances are sometimes seen as backroom dealings and are not meant to sully its mission work.

Spoiler alert! This chapter talks positively and openly about the pursuit of money.

Operating revenues are the lifeblood of a museum. Without money flowing in, the museum will wither and die. Money is an indicator that the museum is providing value to its audiences and supporters. Money can also be an indicator that a museum is serving some of its intentional purposes.

Whatever we are after, somebody else is after it, too. Other museums are trying to attract the visitors we want. Granting foundations weigh among many proposals, anointing only a few. There are lots of other hungry mouths out there, and every cultural nonprofit cozies up to the rich folks. It is a competitive churn out there, bound to get more, not less, intense.

The competition is not just for our commercial, fee-for-service offerings (i.e., our earned revenue). The game may be different but no less competitive for donor attention, government funds, and grants (i.e., our support revenue). They both involve marketing and sales and offering our audiences and supporters benefits they value at least as much as the money and time they spend with us. I think it is all transactional, but then, I define *transactional* broadly as the mutually beneficial exchange of value between two or more consenting parties. Visitors give a museum money and time in return for a visitor experience. Donors give money in return for serving their causes plus a package of tangible and intangible benefits, including exclusive privileges.

When you think about it, all your museum's operating revenues are earned. Not only will a proposal for a foundation grant be hard work, but it must also clearly evidence the hard work the museum does and the results you achieve. I find that independent museums, as opposed to government, university, and corporate museums, must work for and justify every dollar brought in from outside sources. I call this money received from the museum's activities its *operating revenues*, as distinct from its *capital asset revenues*, such as endowment income and lease fees from property you own (i.e., money you don't have to compete for and do work for).

I am not suggesting a change in accounting practice—I'm not that quixotic. The bookkeeping distinction between support and earned revenues must remain, but the museum will benefit if it considers how to manage both kinds of revenue more effectively.

Fundamentally, the job is to sell what the museum has to offer and to offer what's sellable. We create inefficiencies and deny the benefits of scale when we divide the sales job into two or more departments.

Once, philanthropists were motivated by charitable giving, sometimes following family traditions of support for specific nonprofits. Today, the game has become much more complex and much more transactional. Museums now get revenues from private foundations, corporations, memberships, estates, government agencies, nongovernmental organizations, federal foundations, enterprise and cultural district taxes, function rentals, photo shoots, archival and restoration services, tourist taxes, air rights, rents and leases, and, yes, the old standbys—ticket sales, program fees, annual fund donations, and government line items.

Many American museums have diversified their revenues with these new options, but I find that some still rely on the old structures and assumptions. The suggestions in this chapter apply to museums interested in rethinking how they manage their operating revenues.

Although the number and kinds of players has become more complex, I see a sequence of steps common to all these revenue deals: Prospect and product research informs targeted ads and proposals, which attract prospects to negotiate times and terms, ideally leading to closing the deal/selling the ticket with its payment and delivery of service, and, lastly, to follow-up satisfaction surveys. In short, sales.

SUGGESTIONS THAT COULD INCREASE IMPACT

The reality is that no one must visit or give museums money. Museums must compete for every dollar, for every visit, for every engagement hour; they compete with others at the top of their game, and they should count themselves fortunate to attract the audiences and supporters they have. I believe this recognition and humility should underlie a museum's guiding principles, its strategic choices, and the staff and talents they hire. Museums are free-choice service organizations operating in a highly competitive marketplace for time and money.

I believe embracing the recognition that museums must compete could make a museum more effective. How it might be embraced and the benefits of doing so are the essence of the suggestions in this chapter:

- The recognition inspires humility. A museum can't coast on its legacy but must constantly re-earn its audiences' and supporters' trust. It should ration its preaching and maximize its service. I suggest shifting the balance—less attention to changing our audiences and more attention to how they want to change us.
- The recognition widens external perspectives and research to cover and understand a museum's larger competitive marketplace. Museums have been attuned to their community's needs and aspirations, searching for ways that the museum can help. Now, a museum needs a broader understanding of their community's cultural, educational, and social justice needs. Who is out there? Who else offers similar programs? What might a gap analysis indicate is missing? Where might the museum find competitive advantage, and where will it run across insurmountable competition?
- The recognition suggests museums need to choose where and for whom to compete most effectively. Museums can be strategic about where they compete and where they withdraw. Museums may want to serve everybody, but which incremental audiences should you focus on this year? A museum may want to expand its adult program offerings, but is the library already filling that need?
- The recognition prioritizes listening to and paying attention to a museum's most competitive revenue and engagement sectors (i.e., its key audiences and supporters). What do your key sectors get from their museum engagements? What keeps bringing them back? What brings them pleasure and fulfills their needs? Specifically, you are asking your key sectors what benefits they value. Once those are identified, then the museum might include them among its intentional purposes and refine its production and delivery process to make those benefits even more attractive and valuable.
- The recognition emphasizes the importance of sales to the museum's sustainability. In today's competitive marketplace, engagements with a museum don't just happen; they require effort on the part of the museum to pitch and close the deals. Sales is needed at the individual ticket level and for significant donor commitments.
- The recognition reminds us that all sales are about relationships, from families to schoolteachers to senior volunteers to agency heads to longtime donors. Museums have moved beyond mass market attitudes, instead using social media, targeted mailings, phone banks, and greeting scripts to personalize the museum's relationship even with visiting tourists not likely to return. The Net Promoter Score, a

widely used indicator of customer satisfaction, asks how likely your customers are to recommend the museum to their friends. This survey question searches for lasting, actionable impressions. From this successful first start, relationships can be built and developed.

- The recognition urges a museum to clarify and improve the communication about the benefits—not only a fair deal, but an attractive deal, worthy of repeating. Once you understand what benefits your key segments seek, and once you have refined your production and delivery of those benefits, you can work on clarifying how they are described and communicated.

- The recognition suggests unifying the museum's sales, relationship building, and communications with its audiences, supporters, and community under one *external relations department*, responsible for all operating revenues and for all relationships with audiences, supporters, and community groups. This suggestion will be explored in more detail.

INTEGRATE MARKETING AND DEVELOPMENT

A museum's arsenal of development and marketing tactics has increased to deal with a changed and more competitive marketplace for both support and earned revenues. In addition to traditional tools, museums now also use social media, sophisticated targeting, viral videos, online communities, travel programs, angel networks, foundation proposals, cause-related marketing, advisory boards, book clubs, tiered membership programs, corporate benefits, and many other tactics to bring in each year's operating revenues.

The old sharp lines between marketing and development have blurred. Where does corporate membership fall? Who is responsible for Community Day? Who sends out a press release about a big donation? Who pursues a research grant? Who gets credit for sponsorships? Who pays for the tickets handed out to high-level donors?

In traditional museums, revenue responsibility is spread out among several departments, often overlapping, in the visitor experience, or in sales of themed merchandise. Everyone claims credit; no one accepts blame. Bringing more of these separate ventures together clarifies accountability.

I suggest combining traditional development and marketing departments into a centralized external relations department, responsible for generating the museum's annual operating revenue and engagement counts. Many museums already combine these functions, some even calling it the external relations department, but I am suggesting an even closer union.

I am suggesting centralizing a museum's sales team under the external relations flag and rethinking the team and organization as the museum's unified sales force. It might hire specialists for market segments and might have a career ladder, but the whole team would be united by the museum's guiding principles and brand. I believe that an integrated sales force can make a museum more effective.

The combined division would need a strong leader and capable lieutenants separately experienced with the tactics of marketing and development. To ensure unified messaging and purposes, the museum might set two or three specific goals, such as unrestricted contributions, gate attendance, and program participations, for the whole institution to pursue each year, thereby integrating this division's work with all other staff.

When two former silos merge into one operation, the museum should be more effective by combining resources for efficiency of scale and by eliminating redundancies, territory battles, and confusion.

A merger of these two departments will consolidate the talents both departments need, such as proposal writing, prospect and demographic research, hospitality and stewardship skills, event planning, mailing lists, administrative logistics, and many other day-to-day functions.

A corollary suggestion is to include the admissions and telemarketing staff in the department to manage and clarify frontline scripts, customer relations, and data collection.

A larger department can better afford ongoing professional development, resulting in better equipped and more knowledgeable professionals at all levels of the sales department. Friendly competition among a larger sales force may lead to higher revenues when the professionals are recognized for their success. A corollary benefit is that the larger department provides a greater and more diverse set of pathways for each employee to climb.

Most importantly, the merger of the two sales-oriented departments should clarify a consistent message from the museum to all external parties.

POTENTIAL RESISTANCE

Although the museum field makes a valiant effort to reduce class divisions, the separation of development from marketing perpetuates the notion that it takes a certain finesse to handle the wealthy but crass hucksterism to rope in the hoi polloi. This idea that the two cultures don't mix, like silk and polyester, may underlie resistance to the merger, along with normal resistance to change and the potential loss of power and independence.

STEPS TO REFINE AND CUSTOMIZE THE IDEA TO YOUR MUSEUM

To adapt these suggestions, consider adopting some version of the definitions and measurements that follow to clarify responsibilities, identify effective tactics, evaluate budget alignment, and reward success.

The museum's *key service markets* are its main sources of engagements and external operating revenues. There are three umbrella external service markets: (1) the community as a whole, (2) audiences, and (3) supporters.

Start with an analysis of your annual revenue and engagement counts. Where is the funding for the museum's annual budget coming from? And who is the museum engaging? The result of this research might identify the museum's *key service sectors* that collectively account for about 80 percent of total revenues and total engagements. Some of those sectors might be individual supporters, such as a government agency and local foundation; others might be collectives, such as walk-up audiences, members, function renters, and volunteer shifts. Some might dominate in revenues, but be only a blip in the engagement counts, like a federal agency that seldom visits; others the reverse, like free-pass students who may be high in the visitor and program counts but low in revenue.

Once your key service sectors are identified, you can start to research their interests, measure their changing relationships with the museum, and refine how you serve them.

Table 3.1 is not the way a museum's budget appears in its annual report, nor the way departments budget their annual expenses. It is, however, a useful way to identify and quantify responsibility.

The bottom-line numbers must tie out to the official, audited statements for that year. The purpose of this view is to identify specific target numbers to enable measurement and evaluation.

Table 3.1.   Annual Category Counts

	Revenues	Engagements	Sales Responsibility Traditional	Sales Responsibility Suggested
Audiences				
Visits	$ -	-	Marketing	
Program Participations (all other earned)	$ -	-	Education	
Subtotal Earned Revenue	$ -			External Relations
Supporters				
Private	$ -	-	Development	
Public	$ -	-	Public Affairs	
Subtotal Support Revenue	$ -			
Subtotal Operating Revenue & Engagements	$ -	100%		
Capital Asset Income				
Endowment Income Transfers	$ -	NA	Finance	
Other Asset Income (IP, Rents, etc.)	$ -	NA	Varies	Finance
Transfers from Restricted Capital Funds	$ -	NA	Finance	
Subtotal Capital Asset Income	$ -	NA		
Total Annual Counts Available for Budgeting	$ -	100%		

DEFINITIONS 3.1

MONEY AND REVENUES

Money paid to the museum for its operational activities I consider as external *operating revenues*. According to the subjective theory of economics, the dollar amounts are the monetary value of the museum's engagements to its direct beneficiaries. Revenues are indicators of the money the museum's community, audiences, and supporters are willing to pay in return for the personal, private, and public benefits they receive.

A museum's *business model* is the mixture of activities and benefits provided to its community, audiences, and supporters in return for their money, time, and effort.

Revenue sectors are classified as earned revenue, support revenue, and capital asset net income (e.g., endowment, intellectual property, or lease income) as shown in table 3.1.

Accounting practices distinguish between government and nongovernment support as public and private *support revenues*. Revenues for personal benefits tend to be categorized as *earned revenues*.

Endowment income and other *capital asset net income* can be added to the museum's external operating revenues to result in total annual revenues. Museums with substantial endowments, such as the Getty Center (Los Angeles, California), can cover a higher percentage of their operating costs internally, making them less dependent on the external competitive marketplace. Conversely, museums with no endowment must be responsive to their community, audiences, and supporters.

Money paid to the museum for capital projects is investing in the museum's resources and is not considered operating revenues related to the museum's operating activities.

Once the definitions and reporting are set up by finance, then the museum can complete the consolidation of staff and resources into an effective external relations department.

4

Serve Your Community, Audiences, and Supporters

I start this chapter by admitting that I admire museums with a steady and diversified engagement count and flow of revenues. "Steady" tells me the museum provides value reliably to its audiences and supporters. "Diversified" tells me several kinds of revenue sources pay for these values, reducing dependence and increasing reach. "Engagement count" tells me the museum is intentional about counting more kinds of museum engagement than just gallery visits. And "flow" tells me that incoming money flows efficiently through the museum, covering its expenses on time. This flow of money is an institution's oxygen.

If you depend on a mixture of earned income, public support, private support, and capital asset income, as do many independent nonprofit museums in the United States, then the discussion questions in this chapter may help you open your museum's culture to serve and attract your sources of oxygen more effectively.

Over the last five decades as communities changed, the revenue mix for many museums shifted as the sources of museum funding changed. Museums also changed, sometimes leading, but more often lagging, societal changes. Decades in the making and still proceeding, I see museums evolving from preachers to servers . . . from missionaries to enablers, and from authorities to co-explorers. The growth in attendance and earned revenue are the most dramatic changes, and they may mirror the evolution from serving wealthy speakers to paying learners, or, as Stephen Weil said, "from being about something to being for somebody."

The corresponding economic changes to museums may have outpaced the corresponding evolutions of some museums' internal cultures. This chapter suggests three soul-searching questions to help you determine if your corporate culture is in tune with your business model and if everyone is focused on serving your community, audiences, and supporters. You may find other assumed mandates lurking among staff, trustees, and partners.

To explore and reveal how your staff and stakeholders feel about their jobs and the museum's purposes and revenue sources, I suggest discussing a few questions:

- Who pays us to do what we do? What do those revenue sources want?
- To which professional field do we owe primary allegiance? The museum field or our subject matter field?
- What's more important: What we teach? Or what our audiences want to learn?

Only half of the first question may have a simple answer provided by accounting. The other questions raise alternatives intended to open discussions among your staff and trustees. In the end, you are likely to want a bit of each alternative, but which is higher? And what is the spread?

Although the answers may indicate misalignments that limit your museum's effectiveness, I won't try to tell you how to manage your internal culture, much less how to deal with the individual issues when coaching is needed.

WHO PAYS US TO DO WHAT WE DO? WHAT DO THEY WANT?

The first half of this question can be answered by the annual income statements. I like to study a museum's five-year operating revenues to identify the handful of *key customer segments* with *service sectors* that account for most of the museum's operating revenue, like the annual campaign, attendance income, cultural district funds, the Gotbucks bequest, membership, the city foundation, ancillary income, etc. They are paying the bills.

Table 4.1.   The Community and Its Audiences and Supporters

COMMUNITY, AUDIENCES, AND SUPPORTERS

Community is the big-picture, inclusive term. I use it broadly in many ways and roughly synonymous to the museum's markets, cultural context, authorizing environment, city, neighborhood, region, etc. You may serve multiple communities, as does the Emily Dickinson Museum, with its nearby university students, regional tourists, and international poetry fans. Audiences and supporters are key segments within the community that engage directly with the museum. *Audiences* are those who attend the museum's exhibits and programs and are also known as visitors, users, learners, members, guests, program participants, virtual visitors, etc. *Supporters* provide the museum with its support revenues and in-kind services and are distinguished by source of funds into public support and private support and by kind of support into volunteer, partner, collector, and funder.

Every time an audience or supporter individual makes contact with the museum, I define that as *museum engagement*, which cumulatively contribute to the museum's annual *engagement count*. Engagements can be *physical* face-to-face, both on-site at a museum facility and off-site, or *virtual*.

The most common and counted engagement is a museum *site visit*. A site visit is one individual who comes on-site intending to visit the museum's galleries or to participate in a program. Each person-trip is counted as one museum engagement or site visit, even if the trip involves more than one activity or venue. For instance, an admissions ticket that combines two visitor venues (e.g., galleries and garden tour) during a single site visit is counted as one *site visit* but two *venue visits*.

People also come to museums to participate in *scheduled programs*. A museum can hold its programs *on-site, off-site,* and *virtually*—the last two are also called *outreach*.

Any museum engagement that is not a visit is a *program participation*. By this definition, board meetings, volunteer shifts, meetings with grant officers, and event rentals are programs and the individuals attending them are program participants.

You probably have other language for these terms, so you may want to translate my umbrella terms into terms more familiar to you.

The museum's external environment—its community, audiences, and supporters—is diagramed in table 4.1. The framework also recognizes *nonusers*.

What is each of these customer segments getting from the museum in return? This is the second half of the question, and it is harder and fuzzier to answer. Your investigations of the reasons people and organizations give you money is likely to identify several benefits that they value. Can you make those benefits even more valuable? Or deliver them more effectively?

The flow of money and the count of museum engagements are evidence of value. Individuals, families, organizations, and agencies have decided to exchange their time, effort, and dollars for the valued benefits the museum gives them in return. The repetition of these revenue streams over the years is testimony that the benefits have found a place—a value—in the market.

The four categories that make up the museum's audiences and supporters—visitors, program participants, public supporters, and private supporters—are also the museum's sources of potential revenue. A museum with regular revenues from all four *service market sectors* is illustrated in table 4.2.

In table 4.2, the left and right circles are support revenues, and the top and bottom circles earned revenue. This diagram illustrates the need to find the sweet spot: a business model that provides enough benefits efficiently to enough sectors to sustain operations.

Table 4.2. Four Sources of Operating Revenue

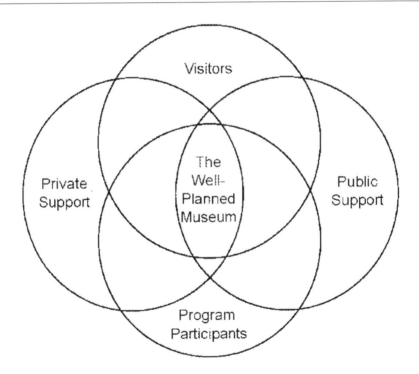

Imagine the four circles sized in proportion to your museum's revenue mix. If you are an art museum, your support circles are likely larger than your earned revenue circles; if you are a children's museum, the reverse is likely. If you compare your current mix to the mix ten years ago, the program participant revenues are likely to have grown.

Once you have quantified your key market sectors by their shares of both operating revenue and your annual engagement count, review them with others in the museum, particularly staff who interact with these supporters and audiences. Are they surprised by the relative allocations? Do they see their work serving these sectors? Does knowing who pays their salaries change their focus? What do they think each sector values from their museum support and engagements?

After a series of such discussions, is staff aligned with who you serve? Do you have a good grasp on what your key market sectors get from the museum in return for their money, effort, and time?

TO WHICH PROFESSIONAL FIELD DO WE OWE PRIMARY ALLEGIANCE? THE MUSEUM FIELD OR OUR SUBJECT MATTER FIELD?

By definition, all American museums are members of the museum field, but each museum usually allies with other professional fields as well. A history museum may see itself as part of its city's collection of history organizations, including history societies, preservationists, librarians and archivists, veterans, and collectors. An art museum may see itself as an active player in the global art world, including art galleries, collectors, art critics, biennales, and art schools. A science museum may see itself as the public platform for its regional science and technology industry. Plus, these museums might also see themselves as part of their local education and culture fields.

To whom does your museum pay attention? Are your exhibit and program ideas driven by an advisory panel of content experts from area industry and academia? Or by what has worked at your peer museums in other cities? How do you define success—by praise from professionals in your subject matter (e.g., scientists, historians, critics, etc.) or by visitor satisfaction surveys? Do you test out ideas with educators or with members and audience focus groups?

Most museums I've worked at seek out and listen to all these inputs to some degree, and different projects have different needs for scholarly guidance. The question is one of degree: Are the experts telling you what they think the public needs to be told, drowning out your audience's interests in what they seek to experience and learn? Do some of your programmers care more about what the critics and authorities think of their work than what your audiences and supporters think?

During the discussions of these questions, you might listen for ambitions to please constituencies outside of the museum's audiences and supporters. Although this can be exemplary—what curator should not strive for critical acclaim?—too much covert striving for external recognition can compromise a program's overt objectives.

WHAT'S MORE IMPORTANT—WHAT WE TEACH? OR WHAT OUR AUDIENCES WANT TO LEARN?

Are you a teaching museum, or a learning center, or an advocacy platform? To kick off this discussion I'll clarify my distinctions and confess my preferences among forms of education: *teaching, learning*, and *advocacy*.

In 1984, when the American Association of Museums issued *Museums for a New Century*, the primary purpose of museums formally shifted from collection conservation to public education. Many now see museums as educational institutions, with the corollary assumption that museums teach. I and other museum professionals have made a further shift from teaching to learning, related to the shift from content-transfer exhibits to skill development activities. Teaching is objective-driven, teachers follow curricula and lesson plans, whereas learning is outcome-driven, what their audiences actually learn.

I gravitate to museums that evaluate their effectiveness by what their visitors and program participants take away from their museum engagements, rather than by what content the museum sets out to teach. Such museums are *informal learning organizations*, along with public television, libraries, and community centers.

Because teaching is objective-driven, evaluation can measure how well the objective is achieved. If the "rivalry of the masters" is the big idea of a painting exhibition, then an exit survey finding that "over two-thirds of the sample audience recalled the competition between Tintoretto and Veronese" is evidence the teaching objective was at least partially achieved.

But because learning outcomes are unpredictable, they are harder to quantify directly. Yes, two-thirds learned that Tintoretto and Veronese were rivals, but what else did they learn? What did their companion say? What will stick? Did they enjoy their learning experience? Will they recommend it to their friends?

For museums seeking public engagements and attendance, I lean toward learning and away from teaching. Teaching feels too top-down for me; the presumption that authorities know some content that should be transferred to the public is a tough sell to the public on a sunny Saturday.

Learning, on the other hand, has always been pleasurable for me, even, eventually, the hard lessons. And it is not just about learning facts but also learning useful skills, evolving my attitudes, developing my identity, and constructing my worldview. For instance, five decades of visiting art museums has expanded my art-world view from the mainstream of western art (i.e., Ancient Greece to American abstract expressionism), to what art historian and critic Terry Smith calls global contemporaneity, which I see as an explosion of visual expression from many cultures in the same time window. What fun! But perhaps not the learning the art museums intended with each exhibition.

Who decides your museum's content and editorial positions? Is your museum a magazine, with each "article" standing on its own staff authorship, though vetted by the museum's guiding principles? Or an agora, hosting content from outside groups, with less filtering by the museum's principles?

Content-driven planning assumes the most important objective is to communicate a specific message to the audience. So many exhibit and program productions start by asking the teachers' questions: What are we communicating? What is the Big Idea? What is this lesson about? This teaching objective may be fine when the speaker with that message owns the cost and responsibility, and when the audience is already captivated by the content. This, however, is not the case for many museum programs.

Instead, I suggest starting with the Big Benefit: What will the supporters and audiences experience of value to them? What outcomes will meet or exceed the supporters' hopes? What do the audiences want to experience and learn about? How do we give them the tools to have such experiences? What other benefits can we offer in return for their time, money, and effort?

Although there are arguments for both teaching and learning as priorities, and museums can choose to emphasize either, I believe that making the third choice to act as an advocacy platform should consider first several prudent limits.

I find that community service museums are seldom funded to be pulpits or platforms for preaching, yet activists expect such museums to advocate climate change, social justice, and public health messages to the public. As institutions operating for the good of the public, a community museum should support such public messaging and do its fair share but while also pursuing its purposes (see chapter 15).

Studies by the American Alliance of Museums (AAM) and others find that museums have been highly trusted sources of information, often above news media, schools, and personal contacts. Activists who want to ride coattails on the museum field's legacy of trust pressure museums to carry their messages. Incorporating such messages in a museum's exhibits and programs anoints their messages with trusted endorsements.

As backlashes on social media remind us, endorsing touchy messages can also erode the museum's public trust—an intangible capital asset that will take years to rebuild. Boards, staff, and other stakeholders can get impassioned by civilization's current crises and urge the museum to act, to be part of the solution, and certainly to advocate for what needs to be done.

If, after considering my cautions, your museum still wishes to endorse an advocacy position, then I suggest three further considerations:

- Advocate if your discipline's professionals agree with that position, but stay away if they disagree. For instance, science museums can advocate for climate action because most scientists agree we need to act, but not for or against nuclear power because there is legitimate disagreement among scientists about it.
- First, walk the talk . . . then, maybe, talk. There is little valor in lecturing the public to save energy if the museum is not doing so first.
- Talk positively. You can catch more flies with honey than vinegar. When we were working on the 1995 IMAX film *The Living Sea*, I thought we should include footage of the damage humanity was doing to the world ocean. The filmmaker, fortunately, knew better, and the film is filled with glorious cinematography that achieves the film's objective of inspiring viewers to love and care for our planet's wondrous ocean.

POTENTIAL RESISTANCE

I can hear the resistance already: "This is selling out . . . pandering to the crowd . . . you might as well become an amusement park if that's the way you think!"

While museums do have higher purposes than serving their audiences and supporters (see chapter 15), who decided on those purposes, and how recently? Note that I emphasize *serving* the audiences and supporters, not entertaining them, or deluding them, or riling them up. The worry that focusing on serving your audiences and supporters will somehow drag the museum down-market might be addressed by my suggestions in chapter 1 to emphasize your museum's guiding principles, rather than your mission; you will not host content that does not pass your values. Your guiding principles are your definition of *museum quality* and your *brand identity.*

An argument can be made for brand purity and for preserving the public's trust in the museum by limiting its activities to some subject or content, such as local history, fine art, science, classic automobiles, or child development. As I have developed brands for museums, I understand the need to police programs for compliance to build the brand, but I don't think science museums must stick with science content, nor art museums with art. Again, brand identity is about character and your guiding principles and not necessarily about your content. Disney's brand identity is wrapped around its family values and is not a commitment to just children's content.

I admit, ruefully, that my suggestion to focus on your highest attendance and revenue sectors seems to fly in the face of my avowed interest in broadening participation and engaging underrepresented audiences. Protecting and even building a museum's revenues may be a necessary step on the way to broadening participation. This Robin Hood tactic stands a better chance of success if engaging diverse audiences is one of the museum's intentional purposes.

Some of the most popular and successful museums are those that teach, such as the United States Holocaust Memorial Museum (Washington, DC), the National Memorial for Peace and Justice (Montgomery, Alabama), and the Rock & Roll Hall of Fame (Cleveland, Ohio). These are remarkable exceptions, preaching messages that attract sufficient funding and followers. Most other museums must attract their audiences by their learning experiences rather than by their teachings.

The counterargument that gives me the most pause is that museums should be leaders and that they should be ahead of the public, that is, beacons setting examples and showing the way. I grant that many excellent museums push their public ahead of public sentiment. Monticello, Colonial Williamsburg, and other historic sites have reminded the public of our uncomfortable past with enslavement. Aquariums have stopped popular whale shows to be consistent with their commitment to animal care.

Here is my twist, however: I think the public wants museums to serve as role models and be "better" than average; the public looks to us for leadership and inspiration. But I do suggest caution about who makes the decisions to lead the public somewhere. Who in your museum decides what is "better" for the public than what your visitors say they want? If you follow my suggestions about governance in chapter 2 and audience representation in chapter 5, then those decisions will be made by representatives of the audiences you are trying to "enhance."

INCREASED IMPACTS AND BENEFITS

The result of discussing these questions should be to sharpen your museum's focus on serving your key customer segments by listening to them and improving the benefits they seek. This should make the museum more effective at serving your community, audience, and supporters, though maybe less effective at communicating your own messages.

To me, this is an improvement and a step in the long-term evolution of museums from unassailable authorities to vulnerable co-explorers.

STEPS TO ADAPT THE IDEAS TO YOUR MUSEUM

I imagine these three questions being discussed in many contexts, from job interviews to board retreats.

Various staff members should be entrusted to capture discussion outcomes and copy them into a sharable document, which can then be synthesized into your culture's prevailing opinions on the questions. From there, your management team will know best how to proceed.

My suggestion to serve your community, audiences, and supporters even above your messages must have been apparent from the start in my word choices and descriptions. I favor museums that serve more than those that pontificate. And, to secure the oxygen the institution needs to thrive, I suggest museums first make sure that they are providing their main attendance and revenue sectors the benefits they seek consistent with the museum's guiding principles.

Part III
REORGANIZE YOUR MUSEUM

Are you organized to achieve your desired impacts and benefits? How does your organization chart align with your audience and supporter's priorities? Are you well-organized to do what you do?

5

Move from We/Them to Us/Us

So many keen and younger minds have wrestled with diversifying museums that I will keep my suggestion simple and start with a confession to set the stage.

In the mid-1980s, all of us associate directors at a large museum were men, as was the director. Those were the days we had secretaries to type our letters.

Our leadership team worried about the lack of women choosing careers in science, and, nobly if naively, we thought our museum should do something about it. We booked an exhibition celebrating women in science, with lots of role models and life stories to entice young women into the field. We started overnight camp-ins for young Girl Scouts, with the idea that sleeping in the museum's galleries surrounded by science and other girls would make them feel comfortable with the subject. We thought that if we promoted science to young women well enough, some of them would make careers of it.

Well, maybe some did, but we men did not understand the real issue: Other men were discouraging if not blocking women from professions in the sciences. Men were favored for prime graduate slots and tenure tracks. Men were favored for engineering and scientific careers. The problem was not women's ignorance of the joys of science as much as it was a patriarchal system that thought men were better long-term investments.

I suspect we would have made more effective programming decisions if at least half of us were women. Now, after four decades of change for women's roles, it is clear to me that a museum that wants to serve both men and women should have both in all its entities—audiences, supporters, staff, volunteers, board, and partners.

I think this principle relates to all categories of people the museum wants to serve: Instead of we tell them, I suggest museums will be more effective if they move toward profiles that reflect the people they want to serve—to make the museum's offerings from us to us. I believe museum policy and programming should be led by representatives of the audiences we wish to serve.

First, I discuss the problem, then make my suggestions for strategies, followed by likely resistance and countering benefits. Lastly, I outline tactics and a sequence for implementing the strategies.

The importance of broadening participation in public museums in the United States comes from the internal need to adapt the business model to a changing market and the external mandates for equity and social justice. In recent years the pressure to change a museum's audience profile has become more intense.

The goal of this chapter is to arm you, as a caring, concerned museum professional, with ways to think about the problem and steps to address it. I suggest analysis, strategies, some tactics, and ways to monitor progress but leave the implementation, policy choices, and goals to your museum.

THE PROBLEM

The patrician and curator-led museums before the 1970s set themselves up as authorities, generously inviting the public to admire their treasures, accept their messages, and absorb their values. My colleague Richard Rabinowitz observes that the Chicago Historical Society was formed in the nineteenth century by wealthy patrons wanting to teach immigrants how to assimilate and pursue the American dream.

Today, on the other side of evolving trends—the growth in earned revenue (1980s), the priority on education (1990s), the Museum Boom (1980s–2008), the interactive, participatory museum, the community service museum, and now, with #MeToo, Black Lives Matter, and the pandemic—we have done a 180, well, maybe a 160. Museums still think they should know a little bit more than their visitors, but we are now willing to learn from them, be guided by their interests, and involve their representatives in decisions affecting them.

The museum is part of the community, while also being an organization of museum professionals and volunteers aspiring to serve their community. I believe greater effectiveness will follow as the two get closer in makeup.

But what does that mean in practice? Closer in what ways? Community makeup has various demographic dimensions: gender, age, race and ethnicity, socioeconomic, and geography/neighborhood. Intersectionality considers how forms of discrimination can overlap. Add psychographic dimensions such as belongers, experientials and strivers, and political and religious divisions, and the goals get confusing. Should museums strive to host roughly proportional numbers in all dimensions?

What's an individual museum to do? As public, cultural institutions, we want to move toward serving all our community's residents and visitors, imposing this social aim on museum planning but also adapting to our changing markets.

This recalibration from *museums of authority* in the last century to what I'll call the *representative museum* moves museums from "We to Them" to "Us to Us." To be

DEFINITIONS 5.1

COMMUNITY, AUDIENCES, AND
ENGAGEMENT COUNTS

What *community* do you serve? How do you define this community? This is a policy question, worthy of staff research followed by board attention and written resolution.

For some museums, the answer can be relatively simple: the local and regional residential market and its schools, plus the visiting tourists. For many university museums, the campus population and its visitors are the community, but for other museums, the answer may be more complex, consisting of multiple communities. The National Museum of the Marine Corps (Triangle, Virginia), for instance, serves at least three communities: local residents, tourists traveling on nearby I-95, and the national community of Marine Corps veterans and their families. It is also a national museum; arguably, it should strive toward making its annual half a million visits mirror the national demographic.

Museum consultant Laura Roberts observes that *community* is a potentially fraught term, especially when used to divide the museum from its community, as in "how do we attract the community?"—as though the museum and its current audience were somehow separate from the community. I have heard *community* used for the people a museum is *not* attracting. A focus group participant complained that she did not see the community in the galleries, just old white folks.

Confusion about what we mean by *audiences* hampers progress in addressing this problem, so I will clarify how I define the term. A museum's audiences are the people its programs engage on-site, off-site, and virtually.

The annual *engagement count* collects all the museum's contacts with its audiences. It is a larger number than the count of gallery visits (i.e., *attendance*) because it also includes the museum's program participations, volunteer shifts, function guests, and more. (See also chapter 12.)

Audiences are people, and engagements are actions taken by those people. Because an individual can have more than one engagement with a museum in a year, the numbers are usually different. The number of annual visits, for instance, is likely larger than the number of individuals who visited.

(continued)

DEFINITIONS 5.1 *(continued)*

The profile of your engagement count may differ from the profile of your audience. For instance, your audience may have more Gen Xers than baby boomers, but your engagement count could tally more boomers if the boomers visit more frequently than Gen Xers.

Each engagement is an opportunity for the museum to capture some data about the individual. Collectively, this data profiles the museum's engagements. It does not, however, profile the museum's audiences. Unless the museum can identify who is making every engagement and ferret out all dupes from the total data collected at each engagement, the museum can report more accurately on its engagement profile than on who engages with the museum.

Hence, I suggest setting diversity, equity, accessibility, and inclusion (DEAI) objectives around your engagement profile, as it is measurable and reflects museum use.

I define *core audience* as the largest cohesive segments within the annual engagement count. This core audience is often the museum's lifeblood. I have worked with few museums that wanted to reduce their core audience; most wanted to increase participation by adding new segments to their existing core.

A museum's *desired audiences* are those the museum wants to engage in the future. The *growth audiences* represent the gaps to be closed between the museum's *current audience* and its future desired audience.

most effective at delivering the programs that will best serve our desired audiences, we should be led by representatives of the audiences we want to serve.

Yet we are museums, and folks expect us to know more than they do. They want us to be leaders and trend setters. So, although we may want demographic parity with our goals, we need to select and praise governors and staff who excel in judgment, vision, knowledge, and professional ability, perhaps evolving what expertise we value.

The problem is that we don't know how to become an economically sustainable representative museum. How might we translate this desire into museum practice? How can we involve our desired audiences in planning the museum to serve them?

However laudable the goal may sound, matching your community profile may be impossible for most museums to achieve and a fuzzy target for museums serving multiple communities.

Some museums want everyone in the community to engage with the museum. Certainly, every museum should remove access obstacles keeping anyone away. All should be welcome. Museums are exploring many tactics for broadening participation, including universal access, multiple languages, free admission, and expanding their outreach and online presence to engage more people from the whole community.

A few museums may be able to match their community profile, but most will run across intractable issues in some of the dimensions: For example, serving all ages is not relevant for children's museums; gender parity may elude muscle-car museums and fashion museums; and some culturally specific museums intentionally focus on a race or culture.

Such issues make it nearly impossible to match all your community's many profiles. Yet the idea that a museum's audience makeup should reflect its community is both righteous and current.

SUGGESTIONS THAT COULD INCREASE IMPACT

Because many refugee Hmong ended up in St. Paul, the Science Museum of Minnesota (SMM) developed programs to welcome and engage the Hmong in building long-term bridges. It was SMM's governance policy choice to increase the share of Hmong in the museum's desired audience profile, and their success in doing so is credited to their professional staff's strategies and tactics and to the Hmong themselves.

Their key strategy three decades ago was to involve the Hmong community in many ways. Although the museum sought their input in programming decisions, the Hmong asked to be involved in the whole museum, and for the museum to learn from them. For instance, the Hmong had experience to share about maker spaces. Today, we can apply this lesson to governance as well as programming decisions: If we want to evolve our audience profile, we should involve representatives of those audiences in governance and staff, as well as volunteers and advisors.

I suggest that the audiences a museum wishes to serve should be reflected in the museum's staff, volunteers, and board, and eventually in its supporters and partners. This section describes a strategy and rationale to make this happen.

This process is about setting policy about who your museum wants to serve in addition to your current profiles. Policy at a children's museum might be to serve children three to seven years old, but the board is considering expanding that range to nine years old. The governing board of an aquarium might vote to shift the current ratio of tourists to residents toward a larger share of resident engagements. The discussion should clarify priorities and why those segments are priorities. Inevitably, there will be segments of the public postponed, because you can't add everyone you may want to serve eventually. Your museum should have sound reasons for this phasing.

It is more actionable to identify specific gaps you want to close as you move through a master plan from your *current audience profile* to your *desired audience profile*. These two profiles must be expressed, ideally, in numbers and percentages based on audience data collected at the start and again at specific intervals. At the end of your latest five-year master plan, was the profile of your audience close to what you targeted?

It is not just about diversifying the audience. Roberts points out that museums need to diversify their boards, staff, volunteers, and partners, as well as their audiences. She suggests that the process starts with whichever group gets traction, as their success will build momentum and confidence.

Diversifying each group is likely to require a customized approach, a sustained commitment and effort, an openness to real change, listening to those who are not currently included, and a willingness to share power and authority with them.

Additionally, museums can use evaluation and visitor research (see chapter 6) to improve their understanding of both current and desired audiences. These tactics are not enough, however. Museums need to change who they are, as well as what they do. Do your guiding principles drive your museum toward community inclusion?

I suggest that a museum should offer different kinds of museum programs to meet the needs of different life and learning styles. The visitor's learning experience in a contemplative gallery is different from how they might learn interacting with a hands-on exhibit or how a school responds to a museum outreach program or how a teen learns in a museum's animation workshop. All the museum's exhibits, scheduled programs, and outreach activities should embody the guiding principles. All should be museum-quality as defined by your guiding principles.

Your program audiences may be many and varied, but all can be totaled into the museum's annual engagement count. I suggest your museum define and use that number and its profile as the basis for objectives, advocacy, research, and planning.

Defining your museum's desired profile is a policy choice, and my suggestion allows the museum to be both specific in goals and general in policy about your desired audience profiles. Specific in naming growth audiences, such as the Hmong in Minnesota or new residents in Florida. General in setting policy, such as for nondiscrimination, universal access, and inclusive language.

Although I have been focusing on the museum's audience, this suggestion also applies to advisory committees and production teams for specific exhibitions and programs.

My suggestion that your board mirror the profiles of your desired audience is advisable and possible only if the board has been freed of its fundraising obligations by setting up a fundraising foundation and other shifts that I suggest in chapter 2.

POTENTIAL RESISTANCE

Political sensitivities surround this suggestion. Any attempt to target a demographic profile that does not match the museum's community is open to charges of elitism or favoritism. Some museum professionals bristle at such criticism, pointing out school and outreach programs, free days, and festivals and culture-specific exhibitions. Museums are free-choice leisure options, and our audiences must choose to engage with us. Museums are places of learning and education, and not everyone wants to spend their leisure time learning. Museums offer what psychologist Mihaly Csikszentmihalyi calls *active leisure*, while many others seek passive leisure, such as watching golf on television.

Striving toward universal inclusion should always be the long-term aspiration. I suggest museums define progress steps toward that goal in each master plan, while also serving their core audiences. We shouldn't rest on just core audiences, because adding more diverse cultures will enrich all.

The decision to shift the profiles of board membership toward some future goal, inevitably puts current board members on notice that the old proportion must change. This may cause resistance from those board members, but if the goal is worth it, even they might understand the shift. I have seen too many boards dominated by old white men running museums that serve primarily women.

INCREASED IMPACTS AND BENEFITS

The most obvious impact of this model is to improve the alignment between the museum's programming choices and its desired audiences. By incorporating representatives of the desired audience in the staff, volunteers, and board, the museum will make intuitive choices that reflect the interests of their desired audiences.

Less obvious, but perhaps more important, is that our ethical consciences will be clearer as we reduce cultural appropriation and replace it with self-expression.

Over the years, as our normalized audience profile moves closer to that of our community, so too will the ties to our community grow in strength as more segments see themselves reflected in the museum's staff and leadership.

At the fundamental level, the inclusion of our desired audiences in planning reduces the museum's risk of failure from well-intentioned but ill-informed ventures where we have presumed to know what a new audience wants without involving them.

STEPS TO ADAPT THE IDEAS TO YOUR MUSEUM

This effort is about the journey toward a representative museum, not the destination, and the journey is ongoing as our communities change and the choices in our leisure market evolve to compete for our audience.

You can experiment at smaller scales and ramp it up as you learn and receive value from the process. For instance, the board may decide simply to increase the number of people of color in the galleries. Multiple photos of crowds of visitors now, compared to the same photos in the future, might indicate progress if there appear to be more people of color in the second photographs. In time, add data collection questions to the admission desk scripts.

Along the way, establish data management principles, such as periodic measurement dates, sources of demographic data, data retention protocols, and internal reports and dashboard postings. The US Census is fundamental to this process because it establishes population demographics, but also because it sets the standards for questions about zip code, gender, income, age, race, and ethnicity that the museum should copy in its own audience surveys to compare apples to apples.

As you develop your data skills, look at psychographics to compare lifestyle choices. Prius and Jeep Wrangler owners may have similar demographic numbers but live differently with different leisure priorities. Some psychographic profiles are likely to have a higher share of museum visitors, and psychographics can help you identify the zip codes where your core and growth audiences live.

Implementing this suggestion is likely to involve some version of the following sequence:

1. Review your guiding principles: How should you go about shifting your audience balance? What do your values say about who you should be serving?
2. Define your community, at least in population demographics and residential geography.
3. Get to know your community in depth. Yes, the numbers, but also what makes it tick, and what's adding value, inspiring dreams, or causing problems. Its needs, aspirations, stories, and characters—a human dimension.
4. Document the profiles of your current audience engagement count, staff, volunteers, and board as your Year 0 benchmark.
5. Determine the profiles of your community now and as forecast for the last year of your master plan.
6. Decide on policy for the profile of your future desired annual engagement count and translate that policy into strategies to reach those engagement counts.
7. Identify the growth segments to be developed beyond your current profiles.
8. Research the growth segments and listen to their representatives: What are their interests and needs? Why might they resist engaging with the museum?
9. Develop tactics and action plans based on this research.
10. Take steps to shift audiences, staff, volunteers, and board to your desired profiles. As noted previously, each group needs its customized approach.

11. Measure changes in your audience engagement count profiles as you go.
12. Identify and refine the tactics that work, incorporating them into museum practice and job descriptions.

You want to go through an educational process to help your board, staff, and core audience understand the benefits of the changes ahead—a wider and richer selection of programs, a museum more closely representing its community, and a more effective museum.

Museum policy and programming should be led by representatives of the audiences you wish to serve. The profiles of your board and staff should represent the profiles of your desired audience engagement count if you want to increase the chances of success. Representation should be balanced to reflect the full desired audience and not just the incremental growth or target audiences.

6

Reorganize the Museum as a Producing Organization

Is there a better, clearer way for a museum to organize its efforts to program its spaces more effectively? Yes, performing arts centers solved this issue long ago, and we can learn from them. The need for a solution becomes more apparent as museums shift from curatorial custodians to program producers.

The recent growth in digital programs is a dramatic expansion of a larger trend toward more museum programs in all formats. The ratio of annual engagements at the museums we analyzed ran about 90 percent museum gallery visits and 10 percent program participations; I think it could have shifted toward the reverse of that during the lockdown months of 2020 and 2021.

At a deeper level, museums have come to realize it is not what they *have* (e.g., permanent exhibits and collections) but what they *do* with their resources each year that draws public engagements. Thriving community museums are no longer fixed attractions but stages for constantly changing programs. "How will we program the museum's physical spaces and digital venues next year?"

This suggestion may not apply to museums serving a changing audience, such as tourists or college students, where keeping the same core story/collection is desirable. But, for museums that seek repeat visits, new programs and exhibitions are needed to keep them coming back.

Programming is what the museum does all year with its resources. Programming includes the museum galleries, exhibitions, education programs, theaters, special events and functions, retail offerings, off-site outreach, and virtual engagements.

On-site programming is how the museum schedules and uses its public spaces. One museum we worked with has 123 public spaces because it includes a school as well as many galleries and theaters. Each space can be programmed for audiences, time slots, operating modes, and business models. A museum's annual on-site programming is the collection of all programs offered in all public spaces all year. Add to that its outreach and virtual programming, and this is a phenomenal amount of programming!

Yet many visitors continue to think of a museum as just its galleries. Museums produce programs.

I use wide, inclusive definitions of the following terms: *programs*, *spaces*, *audiences*, and *supporters*. I use them as umbrella terms embracing categories of more specific museum terms (e.g., *programs* include exhibitions, classes, events, etc.; *spaces* include galleries, web sites, research postings, etc.; and *audiences and supporters* include visitors, guests, advisors, volunteers, donors, grantors, etc.).

The departments that populate typical American museum organization charts—exhibits, education, collections, human resources, development, marketing, administration, etc.—reflect outmoded thinking fossilized during previous museum ages.

There must be a better way, a more responsive way for producing museums.

SUGGESTIONS THAT COULD INCREASE IMPACT

Once upon a time, museums existed to serve and interpret their collections. Natural history museums added dioramas to complement fossil displays, and some exhibits took on lives of their own independent of collection objects. Over the last fifty years, the museum field layered on education, then theaters, then outreach, and then virtual programs. Today, museums use many means to pursue their multiple purposes in addition to collections and exhibits.

Tomorrow's museum structure should own up to this broader role as a multi-platform communicator. The museum is a producer of programs for all its various platforms and for all its diverse audiences. The museum's menu of programs should be unified by the museum's guiding principles, reflecting the museum's brand identity and building on its public trust and relationships.

Museums become *producing organizations* when they align the museum's talents and resources to focus on producing *programs* for the museum's public physical and virtual spaces. The outcomes might include greater clarity, efficiency, creative innovation, flexibility, increased earned and support revenues, expanded audiences and supporters, and continuous community relevance.

The idea is to think systemically about programs in categories of program formats, along with their audiences and business models. This suggestion does not advocate for any balance among types. Digital programming may have soared as a percentage of engagements, and it has earned its category, but school bus tours, art classes, docent tours, citizen science projects, and other older and newer categories also share the list.

A big-city performing arts complex has a strategic selection of stages, each different: a black-box experimental theater; a flexible thrust stage; a proscenium house for touring Broadway shows; maybe a ballet or opera house, along with off-site outreach, touring shows, and virtual performances. Scheduling, operations, and marketing are centralized. When a stage is dark, there are fewer costs. There is something for every audience, with enough variety to permit a few risky bookings along with the crowd-pleasers. The organization is run by an executive director and programmed by its artistic director.

Having wrestled with many museum organizational charts, I suggest a new conceptual model for a producing museum.

PROGRAMMING A MUSEUM'S PUBLIC PHYSICAL AND VIRTUAL SPACES

Imagine a museum that achieves its mission and purposes by using its resources to produce and present public programs. Engagements with this museum's programs produce valued outcomes (i.e., impacts and benefits) both for the audiences and the supporters in return for their earned and support revenues.

This museum inventories all its public physical and virtual *spaces*. Some spaces are long-term exhibit galleries, some are feature galleries and theaters that change seasonally, others are classroom spaces that change hourly, and still others change continuously, like labs and virtual communities. At a given time, each space is assigned a program planned for specific audiences, supporters, and business models.

The museum's *annual programming* is the collection of all programs offered in all its public spaces all year. Most folks assume the museum is responsible for all this programming, whether produced in-house or by others. This museum decides what programs will be installed where, when, for whom, and with what desired outcomes.

A producing organization produces programs for its spaces. These spaces have other names that emphasize what happens to the audiences in those spaces. Roy Shafer called them *experience platforms*. White Oak called them *learning spaces*.

WHAT DOES A PRODUCING ORGANIZATION LOOK LIKE?

The leanest version has only six sequential departments: Research and Evaluation; Administration; Planning; External Relations; Production; and Operations.

These follow the Museum Theory of Action sequence described in the preface: (a) Research and Evaluation identifies community and internal *needs*; (b) Administration, guided by policy governance (the board), decides which of these needs the museum will address and at what scale as the museum's *intentional purposes* and *desired outcomes*; (c) Planning develops *program plans* and *business models* intended to generate those outcomes for the museum's audiences and supporters; (d) External Relations raises the support funds and attracts the audiences in the business models; (e) Production turns the program plans into reality, either in-house or contracted or leased from others; (f) Operations runs the installed programs and takes care of the spaces and audiences; and, looping back to the start, (g) Research and Evaluation measures outcomes and looks at the trends from the operating data and surveys to inform the next decisions by Administration and Planning.

The museum's menu of programming should be unified by the museum's guiding principles, reflecting the museum's brand identity and building on its public trust and relationships. A corollary is that the museum's voice should be centralized at the concept and planning stage but can be delegated to format specialists at the design and production stages. The museum's chief programming officer (CPO) is responsible for planning how the museum will be programmed.

Because the museum's annual program is also the museum's business model, the plan for each program must include its business model, specifically, who will fund it and why (what benefits they will receive). The revenue and expense assumptions, based on research and experience, will be incorporated into the operating budget. For this reason, the museum's chief financial officer should sign off on program selections and dedicate staff to develop the business models. Together, their staffs will decide and plan all the museum's programs and how they will be funded. For simplicity, it should be called the Planning Department, though Finance (part of Administration) will be closely involved.

External Relations generates the engagements and revenues in the business model. This combined marketing and development staff is described in chapter 3.

Production produces Planning's program plans using Administration's scale guidelines, turning the installed program over to Operations to run. The museum uses its resources (e.g., staff, workshops, tools, collections) to produce some programs in-house and contracts out the rest.

Operations is the museum's public face, running front-of-house in addition to volunteers, and facility care. Operations runs the public-ready programs that Production installed in the museum's public spaces.

All departments exemplify the museum's values and guiding principles in their work. All programs are branded or co-branded by the museum, unless credited otherwise.

The kind of work within each of these six departments is similar but different from the other departments, as might be the kind of staff and culture, to better serve that department's deliverables. Planning staff want to be sheltered, eccentric, unconstrained, and creative; External Relations staff want positive salespeople; Operations staff want military order and seek public engagement; and Production wants problem solvers, organizers, and team players. Research and Evaluation wants independence with a touch of academia. Administration wants big-picture thinkers, well-informed deciders, and community champions. With this organization, everyone in each department is doing the same kind of work in an environment that supports that kind of work.

POTENTIAL RESISTANCE

Inertia may be the biggest obstacle to this suggestion. It is a significant change involving disruption of reporting lines, changing job descriptions, and even relocating and possibly redesigning workspaces. Ideally, the benefits of aligning staff according to their talents and clarifying their production roles will offset the difficulties of making the organizational change.

Some staff are likely to operate currently in several camps, alternating their time among Operations, Production, and Planning. One solution is to share appointments, keeping the individual's activities intact. Another, more long-term, solution is to work with individuals to determine their natural talents and their preferred work style and fit them into the department that suits them best.

INCREASED IMPACTS AND BENEFITS

The outcomes of this imagined producing museum might include greater:

- Clarity: Everyone knows what they are doing and how they fit into the museum's production sequence. The department heads responsible for programming, sales, producing, operating, and informing/evaluating the museum report to and take direction from Administration. All programs reflect the museum's brand values.
- Efficiency and Flexibility: Because staff are grouped by the kinds of work they do (e.g., planners, producers, or operators) rather than by their medium (e.g., exhibits, education, or enterprise), they can crossruff and work on multiple projects in multiple media, using similar skills.
- Creative Innovation: The organization fosters peer collaboration, and the diversity of programs inspires cross-pollination. The number of spaces and time slots allow for experimentation and constructive failures.
- Expanded Audiences and Supporters: Programs are planned for specific audiences and supporters. Administration can decide what audiences and supporters to serve, and Research can ask them what programs they want. External Relations can expand the museum's relationships and networks.
- Increased Earned and Support Revenues: Because business plans based on data experience are incorporated into the program plans, the museum diversifies and builds its operating revenues.
- Continuous Community Relevance: By thinking of all the museum's physical and virtual spaces as changing experience platforms and stages for learning, the museum can constantly respond to changing community needs and interests.

All this, of course, should also result in greater community service, more mission impact, stabilized finances, and a more effective museum and staff culture.

STEPS TO ADAPT THE IDEAS TO YOUR MUSEUM

Might your museum become this imagined producing museum?

The first step is to assess whether your museum is heading in this direction already: Is the museum more and more focused on producing exhibitions, events, and other programs?

At the same time, look at the current organization: Is the museum working most efficiently and effectively? Are there confusions, silo issues, and territory squabbles?

The answers to these questions lead to a policy decision: Does the museum want to reorganize to be a more effective producing museum?

If the answer is "yes," then the transition is likely to be complicated, but staff will benefit by being joined with their peers in workstyle and focus, and the museum will benefit by increased efficiency and effectiveness.

Unify the Museum Field

The diversity of museums is both the museum field's strength and our weakness. Museums pride themselves on their uniqueness, and the differences among America's museums are indeed vast. I would never want to take away any museum's distinct identity. Yet even different museums have common components, needs, and aspirations, and much that they can share with other museums despite these differences. This chapter looks at the benefits from working together to unify the museum field for more effective services, advocacy, and impact.

"*Unify* (1) to unite people or countries so that they will work together; (2) to make things work well together." (Macmillan Dictionary.com)

I start this chapter with thanks for everything museums already share. I am grateful for all the ideas, experiences, documents, and other help that existing museums and museum associations have provided. I love this field because museum professionals are so generous and collegial.

Yet, I think the museum field can benefit even more by working together more. Museums could exchange more finished products like exhibits and programs, both physical and virtual, to save money, increase quality, and reduce waste. The whole field could share standards, specifications, and data definitions to strengthen museum buying power, research, and advocacy. I see facilitating such intermural museum exchanges as an opportunity for the museum associations to increase their value to their member museums in two ways: facilitating intermural commerce among museums and moving the whole field from our current loose *collegial community* toward an integrated *professional field*.

We could share more among museums for mutual benefit and to further professionalize the field. True, museums already share operating data, traveling exhibitions, collections, staff, and program scripts, but the process of exchange is often hassled by snags, retrofits, misunderstandings, timing issues, and lack of business models to cover the costs. I wish sharing were easier, so museums could efficiently trade their wisdom and best creations and host more content, saving money while increasing relevance and effectiveness. Further, the museum field could evolve from the current collegial community into a licensed, or at least more-credentialed profession within specific competencies, like our colleagues in theater, film, journalism, and library science. For instance, we have struggled to agree on a definition of *museum*, much less of *visits*, so we don't really know how many museums there are, nor how many people they serve. Public libraries, on the other hand, have such numbers down pat.

Sharing is a process common, but not necessary, to many kinds of museum relationships such as collaborations, partnerships, networks, associations, leagues, etc. I am suggesting establishing deeper protocols of exchange to make sharing in any of these relationships more predictable, simpler, more meaningful, and less expensive.

There are five suggestions in this chapter related to facilitating more exchange among museums:

- Share program components.
- Share standards and specifications.
- Strengthen the museum associations.
- Facilitate intermural commerce.
- Professionalize the museum field.

I admit these suggestions may be difficult to achieve, but the results will address critical decisions facing museum managers: How to change content more frequently, how to compare to other museums, how to manage the field's needs, how to save money, and how to develop tomorrow's museum professionals. All these suggestions involve multiple museums and, in some cases, the whole museum field. To achieve these results, museums need to work together, which from my experience means working closely with gifted colleagues across the United States in productive, eye-opening, and fun exchanges.

Historical barriers to sharing stem from museums' uniqueness and independence, which over time cement separate ways of doing things, making it harder to exchange data, expertise, and content. The first obstacles to increased sharing may be the existing practices—aligning to new shared data definitions may sideline historical data; importing shared programs may idle in-house staff; and certifying job skills may threaten traditional career ladders. Overcoming inertia may incur costs.

Museums will not invest these costs unless the benefits are clear, so this chapter focuses on the benefits from my five suggestions to increase exchange and sharing among museums.

SHARING, COMPONENTS, PEERS, FIELD,
STANDARDS, AND SPECIFICATIONS

Sharing is my umbrella term for all ways two or more museums might use the same resource. The resource might be digital, like a school program script or a data field definition, or it might be unique and physical, like a traveling exhibition that is shared sequentially, or a UV meter borrowed like a book from a central library. Potentially, there are lots of other resources that could be shared in other ways. Sharing is not the same as collaborating, partnering, collective impacting, or unifying, though many of those relationships involve some form of sharing.

Program components are pieces or parts of produced and completed *programs.* I use both terms as umbrellas including all forms of museum offerings, from exhibits to art classes to wedding rentals to outreach busses. Program components might include the props for a demonstration, bases for an exhibit, video introductions, scenery for a display, licenses and permissions for animations, and collection objects for an exhibition.

Peer museums are the same type, discipline, or sector of the museum field; funded by similar business models; operators of similar resources (roughly the same building size, staff size, annual budget or capital assets), located in contexts and markets as similar as possible, and using the same kinds of galleries and theaters.

Commerce, "the activity of buying and selling goods and services" (Macmillan Dictionary), may play a greater role in the museum field than many might want to admit. The $16 billion museum industry not only attracts that much revenue but also spends it. How can we manage all this buying and selling to improve museums?

Collegial community and *professional field,* as I use the terms, are sequential stages of a profession's evolution. The former stage is characterized by informal networks of people employed in similar work, open to newcomers from other fields, and unlicensed. The latter professional fields have integrated definitions, accepted practices, degree-granting university programs, clear ladders, and often credentialed professionals, like doctors, union stage designers, accountants, nurses, architects, and teachers.

Standards are usually principles, measures, and examples, whereas *specifications* are usually more concrete, explicit needs and requirements. "Adhering to the AAM's Code of Ethics" is a standard, and "Fourteen (14) feet clear height" is a specification.

STRENGTHEN THE MUSEUM ASSOCIATIONS

I am fond of and indebted to the museum associations. They bring us together to cata-lyze sharing. Annual conferences, newsletters, webinars, publications, and emails create communities of interest among museum professionals. I and our firm have been members of at least eleven museum associations internationally, but I lose count, and the edges between associations and service organizations can get fuzzy. All brought me together with colleagues who became friends, sharing ideas, gossip, and trends in the breakfast buffet line and over drinks.

Museum associations already do important work shared by their museum members. In addition to online and in-person conferences and meetings, museum associations support our collegial community through advocacy, accreditation, trend watches, publications, member surveys, periodicals, webinars, professional development, and job searches. These are the foundations of museum sharing.

In response to the growing desire to share more, groups of museums have created a bewildering array of associations, alliances, networks, agencies, and boards to support intermural sharing, often with little provision for their administration and sustenance, much less longevity. When two or more museums worked together, they often needed a neutral third party as an intermediary, honest broker, organizer, catalyst, guide, administrator, midwife, or facilitator. And, over the last fifty years, they created lots of them.

- **Museum associations:** The International Council of Museums (ICOM) includes museums globally. Other associations subdivide the globe by continent, nation, region, and municipality. Slice our profession by discipline instead of by geography, and there are associations for art museum directors, science centers, children's museums, railroad museums, history museums, zoos and aquariums, and many more. Then there are the format and professional associations for planetariums, visitor studies, giant screens, conservators, and exhibits, to name a few. These are member-supported and governed; the larger national and trade associations have staff and headquarters.
- **Intermural organizations:** These include funded initiatives serving museums with specific sharing needs on an ongoing basis, such as visitor research standards and specifications (COVES), informal science programs and exhibits (NISE Net), and theater format specifications (DIGSS). MIT's Science Festival links hosts including museums in many cities for their annual street fair. The Center for Advancement of Informal Science Education (CAISE) is a model for other museum sectors to follow for sharing research findings on museum learning. SMU DataArts, started by the Pew Charitable Trusts as the Cultural Data Project, collects operating data from cultural nonprofits using rigorous data definitions and reporting protocols to

generate data required by funding foundations; museums are included, along with orchestras, dance companies, operas, and other arts organizations.[1] All these have some funding and sometimes staff; COVES is administered by ASTC, a useful precedent for other associations.

- **Museum networks** are more ad hoc, informal ventures for museum sharing, typically covering a specific program, format, or exhibit. The museum I worked for joined eight such networks in the 1980s, motivated by sharing capital costs and by covering operating costs with pro rata assessments. Some were just loose listservs, whereas others incorporated new nonprofits to manage significant production contracts for the group, such as the Museum Film Network, LLC. The shareholder museums were the directors who voted on policy, strategy, and tactics. Typically network meetings aligned to conference dates, though now Zoom facilitates intermural sharing and collaboration. Such networks are staffed typically by a manager at a member museum. (See chapter 11.)

Yes, there is a bewildering array of entities already facilitating sharing among museums.

I shy away from suggesting more entities. Instead, I suggest that consolidation and schedule coordination might be a long-term goal. I think the museum field would be more effective with fewer, stronger, big-tent organizations coordinating many sharing initiatives, centralizing standards and specifications, and hosting fewer, larger national conferences and regional satellites, with more virtual forums and webinars.

I am suggesting consolidation at the administrative levels. Do we need all those headquarter offices? Layers of managers? Overlapping memberships and duplicate data dumps? With consolidation, establishing field-wide standards is easier, and advocacy for the field more powerful. The sectors can be represented within an umbrella organization.

In making this transition, the museum field cannot lose the support they bring to new and local museum staff at different stages of their careers and to smaller museums. Regional and metropolitan meetings can complement national conferences by offering services and connections locally that attract newcomers and lower-level staff who cannot afford to attend larger national or international meetings.

This consolidation could lead to efficiencies of scale, which alone could increase service to museums. These larger organizations should also be able to launch deeper, better, and longer sharing initiatives. This should make museums more effective and the museum field more influential.

The corollary to my suggestion to increase sharing services is that museums increase the money they spend on sharing and shared programs and embed the museum economically in its local and professional communities as a guiding principle.

Specifically, a museum's partnerships, collaborations, and exchanges among museums require administrative support and management involvement that should appear on one or more staff job descriptions, as well as in the museum field's backbone organizations.[2]

The Collective Impact Forum, an initiative to support organizations working together for social change, states:

> *Collective impact* brings people together, in a structured way, to achieve social change. It starts with a common agenda. That means coming together to collectively define the problem and create a shared vision to solve it. It establishes shared measurement. That means agreeing to track progress in the same way, which allows for continuous improvement. It fosters mutually reinforcing activities. That means coordinating collective efforts to maximize the end result. It encourages continuous communication. That means building trust and relationships among all participants. And it has a strong backbone. That means having a team dedicated to orchestrating the work of the group.[3]

Further, they describe *backbone organizations* that "pursue six common activities to support and facilitate collective impact which distinguish this work from other types of collaborative efforts. Over the life cycle of an initiative, backbone organizations:

1. Guide vision and strategy
2. Support aligned activities
3. Establish shared measurement practices
4. Build public will
5. Advance policy
6. Mobilize funding[4]"

The collective impact approach is intended to support different kinds of organizations working on the same social problem, and museums are the same kind of organization working on many kinds of public and private needs. Yet the museum field shares the need for a backbone support agency, as described by the collective.

The respected, professional, and capable organizations to expand their backbone services are the museum associations and the federal Institute of Museums and Library Services (IMLS).

To achieve this increase in service, museums will need to increase their support and engagement. A corollary suggestion is to empower and fund the museum associations to increase their data interpretation services. A related suggestion is for fewer but broader associations, resulting in better staffed, truly umbrella organizations.

With strong backbone organizations, the museum field might share more standards and specifications, program components, and intermural commerce, leading to a more unified professional field, as the next sections describe.

SHARE MORE STANDARDS AND SPECIFICATIONS

In our travels from one museum client to another, I likened our planning teams to bees carrying pollen from one flower to another. Museum leaders were interested in what other museums were doing, particularly if they were peer museums wrestling with similar issues.

Peer museums can make meaningful comparisons and assess relative performance for specific *key performance indicators (KPIs)* if they use the same data definitions and understand each other's anomalies.

Our comparisons of museum data were always popular and revealing. We imported loads of data provided by a group of peer museums into Excel tables and visualized the comparisons in charts, which became PowerPoint slides we interpreted for their boards, staff, and funders. "Your membership renewal rates are above average, but your per caps in the gift shop are too low." "Your galleries host relatively high numbers of visitors per square foot, which means you're crowded . . . should you expand?" "Your utility costs per square foot are way high . . . you might ask these other museums how they do it." "Your attendance to population ratio is low, but your city doesn't have tourists like the others."

Such peer-to-peer comparisons were typically shared among six to twelve similar museums in size, budget, climate zone, discipline, and other *peer brackets.* These data comparisons inspired probing questions and informed management decisions, but they were a huge amount of work, one-shot deals, and full of what we called "yes, buts . . ." as in "Yes, your utility costs are high, but you're stuck heating an old railroad station."

Museums can share more when they and their staff adhere to the same standards and specifications. There are some well-developed museum practices that set protocols, definitions, and specifications, such as collection nomenclature, FASB accounting, and LEED commissioning. Several museum associations have established data field definitions, and the museum field has adopted practices defined by others, such as universal access specifications.

Yet, adoption of even these standards is not universal because each museum has its needs for customization, plus years of historic data collected their way. I think museums can do more by agreeing to share more standards.

Many of the museum associations are collecting and sharing raw operating data under a variety of definitions and degrees of compliance by members. Data entry by members can be spotty and inconsistent. SMU DataArts, started by the Pew Charitable

Trusts as the Cultural Data Project, collects data from cultural organizations. Its exacting data specifications increase reliability and accuracy, and DataArts has collected deep data from their submitting cultural organizations, including many museums. The need, however, is for museum-experienced advisers who not only read databases but also know the "yes, buts." This scaffolding of museum-expert interpretation can help museums draw meaning from the databases relevant to their needs.

At a 2007 meeting in Philadelphia convened by American Alliance of Museums (AAM) and the White Oak Institute and hosted by the Franklin Institute, all museum association leaders agreed the field needed to align definitions. Turns out no one was willing to lead the effort, much less give up their existing definitions without strong leadership and clear benefit.

The foundational need is to share operating data field definitions and a glossary of museum terms. Only then can we count national visits per year, keep accurate track of the number of museums and their contributions to the economy, and enable meaningful field research.

Each sector of the museum field currently has its own set of definitions, and some professional interest groups have defined the terms they use but not at the field level. We do not know how many museums there are in the United States because there is not a unified definition, much less a centralized census. The IMLS posted a definition,[5] but even they do not use it in their database of museums. We do not know how many museum engagements there are because we do not have a unified definition of visit or visitor or guest or learner or participant or user.

Under contract to the IMLS, we worked with the associations and with museum data managers to define fifty-nine survey questions and their data field definitions in 2011, with a short list of fifteen to make sure even the smallest museum could fill it in. Museums Count,[6] the museum census, was never approved, so the data definitions were never implemented. They would have established the Museum Operating Data Standards (MODS). The need is still there when the will and the backbone organizations are ready.

Other shared standards and specifications might include open-source designs for a library of exhibits and programs, and specifications for school and youth programs, galleries, theaters, traveling exhibition understructures, lighting and projection equipment, and audience counting and ticketing systems.

SHARE PROGRAM COMPONENTS

In chapter 11, I make the case for sharing more finished programs through *program partnerships*. In this section I suggest sharing program components or the pieces and building blocks of finished programs.

The Digistar Users Group is a model for sharing program components that more museums could follow once their peers share compatible platforms. Staff at one museum with a planetarium or full dome with a Digistar starfield projector[7] can create a show segment (i.e., *program component*) such as a comet flyby or a 3D model of the James Webb Space Telescope that other member museums can download and use in their star shows. These components are exchanged for free among dues-paying members. A commercial market also exists for leasing fully produced programs, such as *Black Holes: The Other Side of Infinity* and *Destination Mars: The New Frontier*. In this example of intermural sharing, program components are shared for free, while fully produced programs are leased for money.

The Digistar Users Group starts out with a lot more going for it than other potential museum groups: The components and whole shows are digital and easy to copy and download; the projection systems are compatible because the supplier makes them to the same specification; the content is geared for educational museum use, and there is a robust global market of users.

To make this model work for other kinds of programs in other kinds of museums, I suggest that groups of potential partners work together to define shared platform and program specifications, production values, content approaches, and business models. If the sharing process is to be sustainable, it will help to have an organization or one of the members take on an administrative or backbone role.

At a macro level, there are already category specifications for traveling exhibitions. The General Facilities Report (AAM, Registrars, 2020) and ILE's Traveling Exhibitions Database (TED) set parameters for spaces and sizes of travelers. But fleets of trucks carrying bases and cases, lights, and projectors still cross the nation, when much of that weight could be inventoried by each museum per a widely shared infrastructure spec.

I suggest that open-source standards and specifications for components will make exhibits and exhibitions better, cheaper, and greener. As we organized the new Science Center of Iowa with its multiple exhibit and program designers, we established technical specification manuals for lighting equipment, computers, hardware, text fonts, graphics, and more, co-developed among all the designers and fabricators. The need for these component specifications was inspired by the Science Museum of Minnesota having to store and inventory more than two hundred types of replacement light bulbs because each of their many designers had specified different lighting brands and types.

In addition to equipment and structures for exhibits and exhibitions, shared program components already include collection loans, scripts, and templates for learning programs, both physical and virtual, presentation slides, and visitor research and evaluation studies. As digital programming grows, so do the opportunities to share digital files among museum virtual sites. Yet I feel these sharing routes could be made more efficient and rewarding to use. It feels like traveling on those old asphalt state roads before the interstate highways. Those of you in the trenches know the problems and costs impeding sharing; perhaps now is the time to address them by strengthening how the sharing happens, as well as adding to the list of routinely shared components.

The clearest benefit from sharing program components is the cost saving, which is most immediate when your museum has been carrying the full cost for independent, onetime production in your operating budget.

Amortizing capitalization among sharing museums also may fund higher quality through economies of scale and an increase in audience numbers, thereby affording better talents and production values.

Building in delta infrastructure (see chapter 8) should ease a space's changeover costs from one operating mode to another, perhaps from a crew call of several hours to a push of a button.

By working more with similar museums, your staff will benefit from peer influences and best practices, building staff skills and knowledge, along with some healthy competition.

FACILITATE INTERMURAL COMMERCE

The museum field's $16 billion industry[8] is largely unmanaged. The AAM manages a few critical aspects—accreditation, communication, advocacy, conferences, standards, resources, and so on—but no one monitors the billions museums earn and spend yearly in the United States. Which revenue sectors justify investment and growth? Which should be transitioned? What field-wide forces need to be addressed?

If rules of thumb for independent nonprofit museums apply to the whole field, then about $8 billion is spent every year on staff and their benefits. This is our profession. How are we treating ourselves? What is the average salary? Are we attracting talent? Are we productive and efficient?

Let's say the other $8 billion is split between local fixed costs like utilities and program costs like temporary exhibits. Part of the problem is that we know little about how our funds are spent, but whatever the real figure, how can those billions of program costs stay within the museum field for mutual benefit? How do we facilitate the exchange of money within the museum field?

Of course, museums need outside influences now and then, but I think museums will benefit more from buying from other museums and museum service providers because they understand museums and may share our principles and purposes. AAM's MuseumExpo is a strong part of this because it brings together buyers and sellers, both committed to museums professionally.

Administrative support for museum networks and grants is another potential growth area, along with establishing and maintaining their intermural business models. With field-wide economic data, the museum associations could champion research and development initiatives and evolve and certify compliance with shared standards, specifications, and templates.

Museum associations are already helping with purchasing insurance and other services, but an even more active purchasing role might publish open specs for admissions systems, monitoring equipment, floor cleaning products, and many other supplies to reflect shared museum needs.

PROFESSIONALIZE THE MUSEUM FIELD

Please understand I am not talking about you. Individual museum professionals are fully responsible and highly skilled. I am suggesting, however, that you and your museum will benefit if we further professionalize the museum *field*.

The evolution from our current collegial community to a credentialed professional field is well under way. In the last five decades, some professional practices have established standards and specifications, universities started museum studies programs, and the visitor studies professionals launched their association, among other advances to our profession. Also, there are now far more museums and museum professionals.

Yet . . .

I had some time to kill after a workshop in Dublin, Ohio, a few years ago, so I drove around the OCLC campus out of jealousy. The OCLC is a global cooperative supporting libraries. They have an annual budget of more than $200 million and a sprawling campus for their headquarters and conference center. They say, "Through technology solutions, timely research, and community programs, OCLC empowers libraries to meet changing needs."

Where is the museum field's thriving think tank, central archive, global advocate, and training ground? Where are the initials after your name certifying your expertise?

AAM's Center for the Future of Museums is the right start because they identify trends and offer ways of adapting them to your museum, and AAM may be among the logical organizations to lead the museum field. But I do not care who rises to lead the whole field as much as I hope some organization does.

The museum field needs a backbone that coordinates among all museum associations, that convenes all museums and strengthens the field. The increased flow of ideas and innovations among all museums will enliven the field; peer comparisons and KPI calculators will make us better; capability certification will improve professional standing; and wider career ladders and professional development opportunities will help professionals achieve their career goals.

POTENTIAL RESISTANCE

I have found few managers object in principle to any of these suggestions; the resistance comes from inertia and from dysfunctional but existing cycles of dependency.

Staff workload is often a limit on the pace of change. It may take time to add sharing and intermural museum relations to job descriptions and more time to see the results pay off. Fortunately, this is a careful, stately journey. We've been on it for five decades or more, and the evolution should proceed thoughtfully but with vision.

There is little point in annual analysis reports or online KPI calculators until more museum managers learn to use data routinely to inform decisions and increase impact. Some managers monitor daily dashboards of data, but others do not yet see the value because the museum field faces a vicious cycle: Spotty reporting of museum operating data means inconsistent collected data, which leads to managers' lack of faith in such data, which leads to making decisions in other ways, which leads to lower priorities in reporting and using data. Meanwhile, the museum field's data-informed cultural competitors and nongovernmental organizations lure away data-demanding donors and TripAdvisor customers.

There may be resistance because, inevitably, sharing and reuse involve learning curves. It is easier to design for an empty, plain box gallery than for one richly out-fitted with mezzanines, projectors, a lighting grid, flexible wall dividers, acoustically isolated pods, and other delta infrastructure. In the second instance, the designer has to learn both the constraints and potentials of the built-in elements. Intuitively, many designers prefer to start with a clean sheet of paper, the so-called blank slate . . . until they see the budgets and deadlines. Then the built-ins start making sense by saving dollars and time.

The diversity of the museum field may resist unifying the museum associations under a big tent. Zoos have different needs from historic houses or children's museums, for instance. These differences justify subgroups, but their shared needs and collective strength justify some unifying, umbrella organizations.

IMPLEMENTATION

As with other suggestions, socializing the ideas among colleagues will first determine if they too see a need for more unity among museums, more sharing, more alignment, and more centralized management of the field. Once enough museum leaders, particularly the association leaders, agree on the direction, then cautious steps can be taken, with the full vision on the horizon.

CONCLUSION

Museums already share with each other in many of the ways I am suggesting. I wish museums could share even more, at least among peers and possibly among the whole museum field in all its rich diversity.

Toward this long-range goal, I offer five broad suggestions: Invest in museum associations to expand their services; move our field toward greater agreement and adoption of shared standards, specifications, and data definitions; share more program components among museums with similar needs; help museums do business with each other and with the museum service community more efficiently and economically; and develop professional practices and certifications for tomorrow's museum professionals.

All these ideas share my passion for uniting our rich and diverse field. Yes, museums are unique, but they also share operations, aspirations, and ideas. I believe museums can help each other by working together more. At a fundamental level, as museum leader Marsha Semmel says, "If museums are to truly make an impact on so many of society's pressing issues, they need to work as an ecosystem to effect positive change."

My suggestions in this chapter hope to make sharing easier while increasing the strength of the museum field. Making it fun may seem a bit of a stretch, but stop to think about the fun you have in the other kinds of sharing you do with friends, with your partner, with family, and with strangers. Sharing, at some level, is about love, and the museum field I love could flourish with more sharing.

NOTES

1. Federal funding from the Institute of Museums and Library Services (IMLS), the National Endowment for the Arts (NEA), the National Endowment for the Humanities (NEH), the National Science Foundation (NSF), and the Smithsonian Institution have supported some of the most influential services.

2. *Backbone* is a term and definition borrowed from the Collective Impact Forum, https://www.collectiveimpactforum.org/resources/value-backbone-organizations-collective-impact, accessed February 10, 2022.

3. https://www.collectiveimpactforum.org/what-collective-impact, accessed January 27, 2022.

4. https://www.collectiveimpactforum.org/resources/value-backbone-organizations-collective-impact, accessed January 27, 2022.

5. From Section 9172 of the 2018 IMLS Reauthorization: "The term 'museum' means a public, tribal, or private nonprofit agency or institution organized on a permanent basis for essentially educational, cultural heritage, or aesthetic purposes, that utilizes a professional staff, owns or utilizes tangible objects, cares for the tangible objects, and exhibits the tangible objects to the public on a regular basis. Such term includes museums that have tangible and digital collections and includes aquariums, arboretums, botanical gardens, art museums, children's museums, general museums, historic houses and sites, history museums, nature centers, natural history and anthropology museums, planetariums, science and technology centers, specialized museums, and zoological parks." https://www.imls.gov/sites/default/files/mlsa_2018_asamended.pdf, accessed February 8, 2022.

6. Museums Count! was an initiative of the IMLS to conduct a census of American museums. IMLS contracted with AAM and the White Oak Institute to research the museum associations and, with their input, develop the census questions and their accompanying data definitions. A total of fifty-seven survey questions were defined in peer review, then sorted into three priorities because most museums would only get a short form. The census was never authorized.

7. Digistar systems are manufactured by Evans & Sutherland (a Cosm Company).

8. Cited from https://blooloop.com/museum/in-depth/aam-annual-meeting-museum-expo/, accessed December 17, 2021.

Part IV
REINVEST IN
YOUR RESOURCES

Expanding museums is so old hat . . . so Museum Boom (1980s–2008). Sure, there are still some undersized museums and lots of historic sites and houses that want to add visitor centers, but few of our large public museums are bursting at the seams in need of more space.

We've spent huge amounts of capital building all this space, yet it is empty and lifeless most of a year's 8,760 hours. Now, we need more value from the space we have.

Invest in Infrastructure, Not New Structure

I am the first to admit that the Museum Boom (1980s–2008) enabled my career as a museum planner—there were lots of big expansions, whole new museums, and billions spent on adding to our national inventory of museum square feet.

I sense that the fervor and funding for new museum structures has cooled, even before the lockdowns of the COVID-19 pandemic closed museum buildings. Now, the national inventory of museum square feet may have declined from a 2019 peak.

During the decades when the museum field was building new space, I noticed a troubling trend. During value engineering (i.e., cost-cutting), when there was a budget ceiling instead of a deep-pocket donor, architects often had to cut the extras that make museum spaces efficient and productive. Too often, galleries originally conceived as fully serviced learning environments capable of magic transformations were reduced to plain-vanilla extrusions of open-trussed space.

Museums have shifted over the decades from bastions of permanence—the rock of history, fine art, and high culture—to alive, relevant community gathering places. Today, a museum's community changes rapidly as political winds shift and youth sets new courses. The British Museums Association found that museums change lives, but to do so now, community museums must find ways to change their content and programs ever more frequently.

At a practical, logistical level, museum staff often face building problems that drive them crazy—too hot, too noisy, door too small, wall too near, skylight too bright, light bulbs unreachable, lousy connectivity, no digital media feeds, and who the hell let them put a six-inch step-up halfway down the gallery? I wish we could . . . have a load-in door . . . have more power and some plumbing . . . fire the designer who put the concrete tree in the middle. One reason to invest in your current spaces is to solve staff complaints about your museum's current space inefficiencies.

Other reasons look forward to what could be possible with investments in productivity: expanded access hours, increased relevance and currency, added kinds of engagements, facilitated flexibility, broadened participation, and augmented capabilities.

In light of these potentials and in these times, it makes more sense to me to enrich and enable the spaces we have rather than build more. The suggestions in this chapter are intended for museums that wish to make their existing public building spaces more productive, more efficient, more useful, and more effective. In this chapter, I offer a big-picture view of the strategy of investing in your infrastructure, define a few useful terms (e.g., *modes*, *scenarios*, and *delta*), offer five tactics, and outline some analysis and planning steps; however, what to do and how to do it must be specific to each museum and involve your staff, museum planners, future users, and engineers.

Yet I recognize it is so much more fun to build new architecture than to wrestle with an old building, and a new wing seems more sellable to naming donors than a refurbishment of an already named but aged gallery.

I understand the seductive attraction of designing a new building by a starchitect, but I have come to realize that more design humility serves a greater good. Galleries and other spaces should be neutrally designed to support a succession of scenarios. The exhibits need to change faster than the architecture. If we are to be responsible stewards of our community's scarce capital dollars, then I suggest we invest our supporters' funds in flexible learning spaces that host a succession of compelling visitor and program experiences.

In talks with staff and in reading their lists of desired changes to their museums, I've heard many reasons to invest in their existing spaces. Some of the categories of facility improvements include:

- Refurbish, redecorate, refresh, renew.
- Bring up to code and professional standards for heat, light, and humidity.
- Improve accessibility.
- Replace aging systems and shore up structures.
- Decrease operating costs.
- Increase productivity and effectiveness.

My suggestions in this chapter focus on the last of these reasons for investing in infrastructure. How can we make a museum's on-site galleries, program spaces, lobbies, and other public spaces more productive and effective? How can they serve more people in more ways at more times more economically? More productive spaces might be able to handle more people, operate in different modes, integrate media and other learning technologies, adjust layouts easily, accommodate new audiences, and serve additional purposes. Adding a sink and a projector to a program space makes it more productive.

TACTICS TO INCREASE SPACE PRODUCTIVITY

Each museum must identify most of its action plan ingredients, but I can offer tactics that might increase the productivity of your existing public spaces, along with some language to help you clarify and communicate your purposes:

- Independent access zones
- Multimode operations
- Delta approaches to changing content
- Changing scenarios: new visitor experiences
- The magic box

Independent Access Zones

Many museums have a history rooted in protecting their collections during a time when admitting the public was a risk to be guarded and rationed. Today, most museums want to maximize access to visitors but are typically limited by the realities of operating costs and local norms. I assume your museum already tweaks your visitor opening hours to meet demand above break-even, so this suggested tactic looks at nonvisitor use of zones within the building by program participants who come on-site to attend scheduled classes, presentations, concerts, social gatherings, reunions, and other programs.

A revealing exercise is to figure out how many small events you could book simultaneously on a peak evening. For instance, how many of the following could you host at the same time: A book club, a meeting of the Churchillians, a barbershop quartet's rehearsal, a memorial service, and a rehearsal dinner? This way of looking at your floor plans can identify a number of *independent access zones*, each with safety, acoustic and security barriers. The exercise may also identify building improvements—new doors, added washrooms, exterior exits, zoned air handling, and so on—that will allow your museum to operate more zones at more times.

Such zones might include one or more program spaces, some galleries in other operating modes, auditoriums, and open spaces, and must include access to an entrance lobby, washrooms, and emergency exits.

The spaces within such zones are likely to have primary functions with purpose-designed layouts, furnishings, and systems. Museum spaces such as a library, a studio, an art gallery, an auditorium, or a school lunchroom pose opportunities and challenges for converting them to serve other functions at other times. Ideally, you can go with the space's strengths—book the Churchillians into the library, for instance. Simple additions may help—add an upright piano to the studio and host the barbershop quartet. Finding handy storage for the equipment and furnishings not used by the current function may be critical to certain kinds of conversions—the tables and chairs filling the student lunchroom need to go elsewhere when the space is used for yoga classes, and a small stage needs to come from someplace to convert the art gallery for a memorial service. Adding storage space can be a tactic to increase productivity.

Consider the gap between your current adjacencies and your ideal adjacencies. Adjacencies are about what spaces are next to each other or connected in some way. For instance, if the traveling exhibition gallery is not adjacent to the loading dock and crate staging areas, then a wide service corridor with good floor loading needs to link them. If you have to carry cash from admissions to the cash-counting room through public spaces, you may have a security risk you could avoid if the cash room were adjacent to admissions.

Independent access zones include adjacent spaces that can operate when the galleries are closed. What new, nonvisitor audiences are available at those times? Who's the potential market for what kinds of off-hour operations? Local non-anglophones may be interested in English-as-a-second-language evening programs. Young adults and seniors may come for social events and regional Scout troops for sleepovers.

These programs need business models. Keeping a museum building open beyond visitor hours costs money and requires staff time (the *fixed costs*) plus the program-specific costs for presenter fees, caterers, rentals, marketing and other *variable costs*. Revenues can come from many sources—fees, subscriptions, memberships, grants, sponsorships, and rentals, for example. Ideally, revenues exceed both fixed and variable costs to yield a net return for the museum on its investment.

Your museum probably does some of these programs already. My suggested tactic is to expand such facility use by strategically identifying alternate use zones, spaces, audiences, programs, and their business models and supporting them operationally by establishing *multimode* practices and architecturally by investing in *delta infrastructure* to facilitate change.

I also suggest managing the museum's programs centrally (see chapter 6) to allow for amortizing some costs, administering the collected business models, balancing profitable programs with charitable programs, and planning strategically to keep enhancing the museum's uses of its building in service to its community.

Multimode Operations

Many museum spaces were designed or modified over the years to do one thing well. These choices, however, constrain today's managers from using the space for other purposes. Investing in public spaces so that they can serve multiple uses will make them more productive, though I recognize an insensitive expansion of capability might erode the effectiveness of the original purpose.

Converting a space from function A to function B or, as I call them, from *operating mode* A to mode B, can be as simple as pushing a preset button or as complex

Table 8.1. Multimode Operations: Assumes an Open, Multipurpose Gallery

Modes	Active School Weeks	Slow School Weeks	Summer and Holiday Weeks	Total Yearly Weeks
	30	7	15	52
Student Group Mode				
Public Visitor Mode				
Cultural Center Mode				
Special Event Mode				
Subtotal Visitor Hours				
Program Mode				
Food Service Mode				
Camp-in Mode				
Meeting Mode				
Function Rental Mode				
Subtotal Program Hours				
Preparation and Maintenance Modes				
Shift and Setup Time				
Dark Time				
Subtotal Staff and Dark Hours				
Total Hours/Year	5040/yr	1176/yr	2544/yr	8760/yr

as calling a crew to work through custom transformation instructions. Once your museum decides it is beneficial for a space to be able to convert regularly from mode A to mode B—and possibly to C, D, and E, while you're at it—then it may be prudent to invest in infrastructure that facilitates these mode transformations. Lighting preset panels, room dividers, blackout curtains, new storage hideaways, plentiful power distribution, overhead grids or catwalks, sinks and drains, built-in media, sound and light-lock entrances, catering rooms, and other investments can empower *multiple-mode operation.*

A simple example: A museum library built around a central worktable and chairs can operate in Library Mode during its public hours, in Meeting Mode in the evening, and in Maintenance Mode at night. The conversion from Library Mode to Meeting Mode involves staff turning off the lighting in the stacks, lowering the projector and screen, leaving, and locking the front door. The Churchillians' higher-level membership cards unlock the door and log their attendance. At the end of Meeting Mode, all room lights are turned off and the motion-activated work light system is set for Maintenance Mode.

Other spaces may offer features that lend themselves to other modes, and new audiences may also suggest other modes. Your museum might offer Group Tour Mode, Function Rental Mode, Exclusive Sponsor Mode, Teacher Institute Mode, School and Youth Group Modes, Presentation Mode, Food Service Mode, Valuable Object Mode, Cultural Center Mode, Workshop and Studio Modes, Camp-in Mode, plus the other modes suggested by your needs, spaces, and audiences.

I suggest that formalizing operating modes and their transformations for selected spaces will help a museum manage the expanded use. Once you define some modes, you can count the uses of each mode, the number of participants per mode, and the number of transitions from mode to mode. This data will point to mode transitions worth improving.

Table 8.1 is a template you can adapt to imagine your busiest, most fully realized multimode space, and then you can select, prioritize, and phase your choices as needed.

Delta Approaches to Changing Content

The letter *delta* is the Greek symbol for change. If you start using *delta* as a positive descriptor as I do, as a compliment even, as in "That flexible design is very delta," "Adding a grid makes the space more delta," and "Endowment is a delta type of philanthropy," then your museum's commitment to facilitating change will grow.

The delta concept has many uses and tactics. I believe most museum galleries should incorporate delta tactics for change, even if it is only a provision for updating labels. Some delta tactics include:

- Gradual evolution to update long-term exhibit investments, like replacing a few exhibits in a hands-on arena or in an iconic dinosaur hall.
- Staff and volunteer floor programs are labor intensive, but they are easily changeable aspects in exhibit galleries.
- Reinterpreted exhibits, particularly collections, by a curator with new labels and lighting.
- Rearranging a kit of parts and filling the modules with new contents, like showcases and contemplative galleries.
- Specialized galleries with long-term exhibit structures can change in large, marketable ways by installing new exhibits and environments on those structures.
- Open, neutral spaces geared for traveling exhibitions.
- New shows, films, and demonstrations in a museum's theaters and program spaces.

Each learning space can have one or more of these *delta change tactics* assigned and built into the infrastructure—the experience platform[1] layer—to facilitate changing content.

I recognize, however, that some few spaces in a community museum might remain unchanged for good reasons. Iconic spaces, such as the walk-in heart at the Franklin Institute (Philadelphia, Pennsylvania) and the Rothko Chapel (Houston, Texas), and curricular exhibits, such as the time line at the History Colorado Center (Denver, Colorado), stay constant because passionate fans and returning teachers demand it.

Changing Scenarios: New Visitor Experiences

Before I joined the museum world, I designed scenery and lighting in the theater. When I first worked inside a large museum in the 1980s, I was shocked . . . shocked to find how difficult, expensive, and time-consuming it was to change over a museum gallery—scads of meetings, millions of dollars, and years of implementation. In the theater, a mainstage production closed Sunday afternoon and by Tuesday night the next show was up. Built-in infrastructure and professional training enabled this conversion speed. Every proscenium theater has at least a main and fire curtains, torm, boom, beam and first-electric lighting positions, an overhead grid, and an inventory of audio and lighting equipment run by sophisticated programmable controllers. As a professional, I was trained in how to use these, and I came to rely on finding them in every proscenium theater I worked in, plus or minus lots of other bells and whistles.

Museum galleries are not theaters, and the parallel breaks down because museum professionals are handling collections, not scenery, and visitors are up close, not far away in the dark. Even well-equipped traveling exhibition galleries require weeks to change exhibition scenarios. Yet there are principles from the theater model that can be applied to the gallery spaces that management wants to change more easily, frequently, or economically. I'll start with the useful distinction in the theater between the *stage*, with all its infrastructure for change, and the *play*, full of its unique content and meaning.

I have been interested in finding ways to make just enough change to a gallery that a repeating visitor sees it as a new experience. I call this scale of gallery change *scenario change*, like the theater's ability to change from one play to the next play.

I suggest that planning the renovation of a significant museum space should start with "What scenarios might we want to install in this space when we're done improving it? And what can we build in now that will support these scenarios?" Perhaps you want to dedicate the gallery to Renaissance paintings, so adding focused lighting systems, wainscoting, and fabric wallcoverings may enrich many different hangings from the collection. Perhaps you want a succession of water-based exhibits, so adding washable floors, drains, and water supplies at the start makes sense.

Table 8.2. The Delta Gallery: Two Layers in Comparison

Delta Gallery	Scenario
The Stage	*The Play*
Built-in	Changeable
Capital budget	Operating budget (goal)
Funding theme	Promotion opportunity
Background	Foreground
Neutral or iconic	Visually striking
Platform designer	Exhibit/media designer
Code engineering	Unlicensed designers
Building contractor	Exhibit fabricator
Built in place	Built off-site

The *delta gallery* is an approach to adding infrastructure to facilitate scenario and other content change. The change from one *scenario* to another can be faster and more economical if the museum can invest in *delta infrastructure* to facilitate change. The approach tries to reduce the cost of each change by building in long-term support for changing the exhibits, theater shows, and programs more economically. The layers of a delta gallery are illustrated in tables 8.2 and 8.3.

Table 8.3. Delta Museum: Layers and Rate of Change

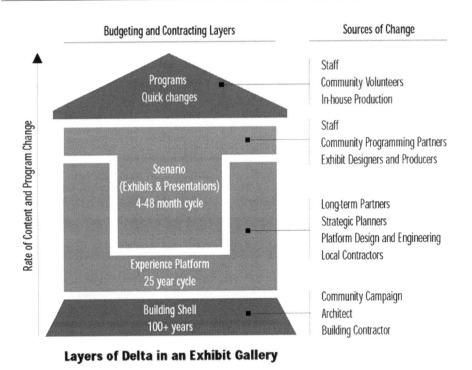

Layers of Delta in an Exhibit Gallery

A Magic Box

Just as it useful to imagine all the operating modes and scenarios you might want in table 8.1, it is illuminating to think up a fully delta gallery so you can decide which aspects are your priorities.

What I call a *magic box* I have also called a feature center, a changing exhibition gallery, and an exhibition transformer, reflecting slightly different formats for different museums. The equivalent stage in a performing arts center is its experimental theater, typically a black box full of flexible systems and moveable seating risers.

My ideal magic box is a large, rectangular open gallery of 6,000 to 12,000 net square feet. At least 16-feet clear height, but 20 feet would fit more shows. The floor, covered in carpet tiles, has a grid of embedded utility boxes. Overhead catwalks, lots of lighting, and media equipment on pipe grids with power and signal distribution cover the space. Lighting and media control systems enable changing presets instantly from disco to Devonian rain forest. Everything overhead is flat black, but the sound-absorbent walls and carpet are neutral taupe. Two nearby public doors allow for entrances and exits to be routed by entrance setups and exit gift shop spaces with a well-signed connection back to the museum's main circulation. On the other side of the space, a load-in gate allows crates to roll in and out. Ample floor-loading allows forklifts with crates to roll across the space. An inventory of flexible wall panels stack at one end and allow the open space to be partitioned in many ways, with electrical and data distribution throughout.

You can add to this wish list—collection-quality HVAC? Compressed air? Ceiling suspension points?—to complete your museum's ideal fantasy space. Then you can become realistic and select the elements where the need is greatest and the return clearest.

POTENTIAL RESISTANCE

Frankly, my suggestions are not as exciting as a flashy new wing filled with new permanent exhibits. Raising money for content-neutral infrastructure might be similar to raising money for endowments; both are long-term additions to the museum's permanent capital providing continuing returns, unlike permanent exhibits that soon start to fade.

Increased infrastructure can increase operating costs and skill expectations, and the return-on-investment calculations must assess both the savings and the cost. Study should precede purchase of sophisticated control and media systems. Technology may enable dramatic mode changes at the push of a button, saving hours of trained staff time daily, but can require annual maintenance contracts and someone in the building who knows how to program and hack the system when needed.

Some may fear that enabling change compromises a space's prime function. Is a space that does two or more things pretty well better than a space that does one thing very well? Do multifunctional spaces compromise each function? When faced with a screw, I reach for a screwdriver and not a Swiss army knife. But I'm lucky enough to have screwdrivers, knives, punches, scissors, corkscrews, and rasps at hand. But if all I have is one tool, I'll take the Swiss army knife.

Some donors, exhibit designers, and teachers are interested in permanent exhibits because of their longer impact, greater budgets, and constant message. Museum leadership needs to decide how much gallery space should be long term and how much should change periodically.

The most intractable resistance to investing in infrastructure may be simply that such projects can be complicated, cross-silo, unexciting, and far-future payoffs. More reason for visionary leaders and funders to champion them to increase the museum's effectiveness in the long term.

INCREASED IMPACTS AND BENEFITS

The impact of these operational and technical suggestions on a museum's impact and service to its community can be enormous. Finding ways to open more of the building for more hours can serve new audiences coming for new kinds of experiences. By finding automated and low-staff ways of changing operating modes regularly and scenario changes periodically, the museum can change its offerings more frequently, increasing relevance and enabling quick-response programs.

Ideally, capital investments in long-term infrastructure should result in operational savings, both in cost and staff time. After the investments are complete, the museum should be stronger and livelier, with more ways of serving its community. Operationally, the museum should be more flexible, relevant, profitable, and effective.

STEPS TO ADAPT THE IDEAS TO YOUR MUSEUM

Who do you talk with about making your spaces more productive? I suggest starting with conversations with staff, specialized users, and engineers.

Floor and facility staff are aware of their building's limitations and frustrations, as are docents and guards. They know where storage is most needed, where traffic jams occur, and where existing systems are broken or inadequate. They may also have solutions. From these conversations you can develop a facility wish list and database. Encourage all problems and solutions, because you can clump and prioritize later.

Ask potential users what they might need. Collection specialists, event planners, camp-in coordinators, tour guides, climate engineers, and security managers will identify what investments will increase use and revenue. For instance, an event planner will tell you that you need a separate bride's room to host most weddings.

DEFINITIONS 8.1

GROSS AND NET SQUARE FEET

In the United States, size is typically reported as *net square feet (NSF)* or *gross square feet (GSF)*. *Net* is the usable space, and *gross* is that plus wall thickness, service ducts, utility rooms, circulation, and other needed functions. The distinction is far more detailed and requires attention to make sure you are not totaling different kinds of measurements or double-counting service functions—I suggest working either all in NSF or all in GSF. An efficient museum building can have a *net-to-gross ratio* as low as 1.25, whereas a spacious building with open spaces and dramatic circulation can run as high as 2.0.

If you are contemplating construction that requires a permit, then you should talk with licensed engineers. A big job or local codes may require an architect to head an architecture and engineering (A&E) team, but the kinds of infrastructure investments suggested in this chapter are technical and not aesthetic. Structural, electrical, and systems engineers will tell you if doors can be punched through walls, power distributed to grids, and controls added to zones.

As usual, start planning with research into current conditions, followed by discussion and consensus-building that leads to defining your desired future conditions. This three-step start-up process appears often in my other suggestions. Do some scenario brainstorming: What different scenarios might we someday want to install in these spaces? Once you know what spaces you have and how you want to improve them, then you can develop an implementation plan, schedule, and budget. I'll outline some starting steps; after that, each museum can best determine its own action plan.

I suggest starting with a *Space Use Analysis* to understand how your museum is currently using the spaces you have. You may find *architectural programs* in your files listing each space with its name, number, and size.

1. Verify and update your architectural program and enter its list of all spaces and their square foot size into Excel.
2. Find floor plans and draw simple versions on regular graph paper (for discussion only).

3. Color-code floor plans according to function and tally the square feet of each color in the Excel worksheet.

4. Are there *independent access zones* (contiguous spaces) on these floor plans that might be available to the public when the rest of the museum's public spaces are closed?

5. Calculate the percentage of square foot given over to each function. What share of your building is public, semipublic, or nonpublic support space? Within public, what share are galleries, theaters, program spaces, and lobbies?

6. Determine the code occupancy of each space (i.e., potential momentary capacity) and estimate the actual yearly throughput of each space. Calculate how many *full-house equivalents* that space hosts per year.

7. Note qualitative factors for the main spaces, such as extra operating costs, large windows, flooring, and lighting systems.

8. Assess the ease of changing the content in each space (i.e., its *degree of delta*). Theaters, painting galleries, and open traveling exhibition galleries have a high degree of delta, whereas tunnels with dioramas, historic rooms, or settings for large sculptures tend to be lower in delta because they are harder to change.

9. If possible, collect architectural programs from your peer museums and from museum publications,[2] and calculate how their percentages compare to yours.

10. Analyze this research. Start with the obvious, big-picture observations. Do the percentages currently assigned to each function seem out of whack? What spaces might shift function to adjust the balance? Are there spaces that get little use on a yearly basis? Are too many of your spaces hard to change? Might evening and night zones be expanded?

11. Summarize your research and analysis into a discussion document or presentation shared with the museum's managers.

Informed by this research and analysis, the museum is armed to make decisions about which spaces to invest in upgrading, resulting in a *Space Use Recommendation*. This perspective on investing in infrastructure to increase the productivity of selected spaces can be integrated with the museum's routine needs for renovations and repairs into its *Facility Master Plan*.

CONCLUSION

I encourage fellow museum professionals to add more ways to make a museum's public spaces more productive. This is one of the greatest creative challenges facing museums today: How can museums get more use and revenue from their costly buildings? How do we move from typical museum hours of 7/6 (42 hr/wk) closer to 24/7 (168 hr/wk)? Are there other audiences with other needs at different times? How do we wring more uses out of our existing spaces and change their content more frequently? How do museums change as quickly as their communities?

Although the suggestions in this chapter can be implemented on their own, they will be more effective if combined with the ideas in other chapters, as described in the book's last chapter.

NOTES

1. I credit this term to the late Roy L. Shafer.

2. Section 84: "Space Use Analysis" in my *Museum Manager's Compendium* (2017, Rowman & Littlefield) has several sample programs and comparisons.

9

Leverage Existing Assets

I used to be envious of museums that had some "lucky" asset generating found money every year. Here are four of my favorites, both because of the amount of money generated and the policy questions raised:

- The Emily Dickinson Museum (Amherst, Massachusetts), with its two historic structures, limited attendance, small staff, and six-figure budget, received a bequest of $22 million in 2019 from the estate of a deeply committed board member. The conditions of the bequest put pressure on the museum to raise other funds.[1]
- The Miami Children's Museum, located in a starchitect building right on the causeway linking Miami and Miami Beach, rented out its superb visibility to motorists to an electronic billboard company that pays them six figures annually. They have some control over what is advertised, but should a museum show ads?[2]
- The Maryhill Museum of Art (Goldendale, Washington) sits on a bluff overlooking the Columbia River Gorge. High up on the ridge behind the historic mansion and its tasteful addition, the wind howls along the Gorge. The Maryhill has leased the ridgeline to a wind farm operator, and the ridge is lined with many twirling turbines.[3]
- The New York Hall of Science (Flushing Meadows, New York) has a large parking lot adjacent to where the US Open is held for three weeks. Using this for paid parking and staging during the tennis matches is a revenue bonanza for the city-owned museum. Although this use may compromise regular museum access, the matches fall mostly in the hall's slow season.[4]

None of these revenue sources is the museum's core business. None of them requires the museum to do much of anything, besides collect the money and maintain the asset. None of them is what I have been calling the museum's *activities*, responsible for generating the museum's *operating revenues* and its *engagement counts*. Rather,

CAPITAL ASSET INCOME; TANGIBLE AND
INTANGIBLE ASSETS

A museum's long-term resources—its buildings, land, collections, fixed
exhibits, endowment, intellectual property, and reputation—are its *capital
assets*, and when those assets generate income, I call that *capital asset
income*, as opposed to *operating income* from audiences and supporters.
The former comes from what you have; the latter from what you do. Part
of the appeal of capital asset income is that you usually work less for that
kind of money and have more latitude on what you spend it on.

Endowment income is the simplest example of capital asset income:
You invest money in a portfolio of holdings that generates interest and
dividends every year. Other examples include lease rentals on property
owned by the museum and intellectual property rights on content owned
by the museum.

Tangible assets are physical and measurable and include land, buildings, furniture, fixtures, collections, and financial holdings. Tangible
assets can carry a monetary value in the marketplace.

Intangible assets do not exist physically, but they have the potential to
generate revenue, such as a copyright to a song and a brand's premium.
A museum's intangible assets might include its reputation or brand, its
intellectual property, its expertise, and its prestige.

these annual money flows I call the museum's *capital asset incomes*, meaning money
you earn from some permanent, capital resource you own and are not otherwise using.

They are also what I will call in this chapter *nontraditional revenues*, as opposed
to *traditional revenues* that appear frequently in museums I've worked with. As your
museum likely has considered leveraging traditional museum lines of business, I will
touch on them only briefly, with a checklist reminder, and then spend the rest of this
chapter exploring how your museum might develop nontraditional revenues.

TRADITIONAL SOURCES OF MUSEUM REVENUE

There are many reasons to think first about leveraging traditional sources of museum
revenue, such as admissions, annual funds, memberships, and grants, before exploring nontraditional sources. Your museum is probably already involved in many of

the ones I list; you have in-house expertise in those businesses, you have existing customers, you have a staff structure already, you know the vendors and suppliers, your museum peers can share their wisdom, and these traditional sources are closest to a museum's core business. These business lines are in your wheelhouse.

Use table 9.1 as a checklist. How many of these are you doing already? Which ones would you like to add or grow? Which do you expect to decline? Which potential growth sources might return the most net?

Managing these, however, is your traditional business, so I will move on to the nontraditional revenue, because that, by definition, is new territory to explore.

Table 9.1. Traditional Museum Revenue Sources

Visitor-Based Earned Revenues	*Private Support-Based Revenues*

Admissions revenue from visitors
  Museum galleries
  Feature experience(s)
	Donor bequests and gifts
	  Annual campaign
	  Memberships (higher level)

Visit enhancement options (e.g., audio guides)	Fundraising events
Parking fees	Private foundation grants
Retail shop and food service revenues	Corporate membership
Memberships (basic)	Corporate sponsorships
Program-Based Revenues	*Public Support-Based Revenues*
Preschool	City
Charter or magnet school	County
Facility and function rentals	State
Fee-based public programs (lectures, courses)	Federal
Fee-based school and youth group programs	Public foundation/agency grants
Festival and event fees	*Asset Income*
Camps	Lease payments from tenants
Ceremonial, memorial, and honorary events	Intellectual property income
Curatorial and conservation services	Endowment income
Grant-funded educational programs	Endorsements
Teacher professional development programs	
Travel programs	
Physical outreach programs	
Research fees and grants	
Virtual programs (web, social media, etc.)	

NONTRADITIONAL SOURCES OF MUSEUM REVENUE

The four nontraditional windfalls at the top of this chapter were not just about luck. There is a process, a path to take to discover and leverage your museum's unrealized and unexplored capital resources. This chapter suggests some of the stepping-stones along that path; I leave to you the steps that depend on your unique context and assets. If you are avoiding these potentials because they are outside your comfort zones, perhaps it's these comfort zones that are keeping you from being more effective. Maybe you won't discover a pot of gold at the end of the path, but you won't know until you look.

1. *Assess board encouragement*

I have known too many directors who got in trouble by getting too far in front of their boards. Hence, my first step is to open this process to the board to seek their guidance on policy questions:

- Are we open to business lines outside of our core business if they don't interfere?
- How would we use a new, steady source of unrestricted income? How hungry are we?
- Are we open to long-term contracts with third parties to use one or more of our assets in return for revenue, provided the use does not materially interfere with our core businesses or violate our guiding principles?
- What is our tolerance for risk about potential damage to our capital assets, both tangible and intangible? How might we insure or mitigate any such risks?

If the answers to this first round of policy questions are "No, No, No, and None," stop right here and don't waste your time. But if your board is open, then move along to the next step; you will return to the board later with more specific policy questions.

2. *Inventory potential capital assets*

The next step is to inventory potential capital assets. You are looking for unrealized, underused, underperforming, or underdeveloped assets. Start with simple lists of tangible and intangible assets and gaps in your community's services.

Some of the *tangible assets* will be listed on the museum's balance sheets and in your insurance coverage. The list should include your land, building, heavy equipment, collections, financial holdings, and other physical resources. Are any of these unused? Are any unused some of the time? Are there times and access for others to use them too? Can any of these be used as collateral for cash loans? Museums often have far more collection objects in storage than on view—can some of these be rented, as does the deCordova Museum (Lincoln, Massachusetts) that places artworks in local corporate offices? Are there any empty offices you might rent out? The Museum of Modern Art (New York) leases its property and air rights to commercial developers, lending their prestige to apartment dwellers.

Museum prestige shifts this inventory task to the museum's *intangible assets*, which you should also list. Museums are highly respected as reliable sources of information; they are often prestigious cultural landmarks, recognized and admired by many. How do you monetize this asset of your spotless reputation without tarnishing the museum's brand identity? By carefully building on and demonstrating your guiding principles and certainly not by violating them. For instance, the ridgeline of wind turbines above the Maryhill Museum of Art exemplifies its commitment to environmental conservation, also evidenced by their LEED Gold new wing.

Contemplating Moshe Safdie's architectural model for a proposed new museum we were planning, the citizens in focus groups wanted to honor important achievements there, like winning sport teams, returning Olympians, and student debate winners. In addition to all the museum's normal offerings, they valued the prestige of being associated with the museum.

Symbolic value is related to and leveraged by prestige. Museums can act as symbols for their community. The Tech Museum of Innovation (San Jose, California) is a symbol for Silicon Valley. The Boott Cotton Mills Museum is a symbol for Lowell, Massachusetts, and its historic past. The Arthur M. Sackler Museum (Harvard University, Cambridge, Massachusetts) is symbolic of the Sackler's economic success. Each of these museums stands for something in its region. Even people who never engage directly with the museum can read the museum's symbol. Your museum is likely to be symbolic to some degree because art museums symbolize a city's cultural ambitions, and industrial history museums symbolize its technology heritage. What is your museum's symbolic value? Can you leverage this asset?

Because intangible assets are harder to identify, brainstorm with staff, board, civic leaders, and museum veterans to develop your museum's list of intangible assets along with possible ways of leveraging them. Ask participants: What intellectual property do we control? Do we have expertise and extra capacity useful to others? Who might it be valuable to and why? What is the added value of hosting something here at the museum? When does hosting become endorsement? How do we protect our reputation? What is our line between sponsorship and advertising? Can we increase our partnerships to our mutual benefit? Are there any transformative bequests out there among our stakeholders?

You may find it informative to conduct a *gap analysis* of your community to identify missing services and products usually found in other, similar communities. Does the community lack a children's museum? Do after-school teens need constructive activities? Does the city's master plan call for broadening participation?

Ideally, the synthesized results of these inventory tasks produce a short list of *candidate development projects*, each proposing a new, revenue-generating use of an existing museum asset, coupled with a notion about why someone would pay for it in a *conceptual business model*.

3. *Research and concept development*

Investigate precedents for the short-listed candidates: Are there strings on how you can use this asset? What's your history with it? How might it fit within your guiding principles? Who else does this? What is their experience and data? What do your potential revenue sources think? Does it require capital? What risks are faced?

Might exploiting an asset expose the museum to new taxes, such as local sales taxes and unrelated business income tax? If so, how does this affect the business model?

Be open to both positive and negative findings as you further winnow down the list to two or three candidate developments. Then, collaborate with others to define *concept development plans* that report the research and connect it to a conceptual description and preliminary operating and economic model in a handful of slides. For each candidate, state the potential returns and museum commitments. Bring the final versions back to the board for further guidance.

4. *Board policy guidance*

Board members will have opinions about which candidate is most promising . . . and which most inappropriate for the museum. This is an excellent time, I find, to coalesce leadership around a set of priorities and build buy-in and anticipation.

But it is also a time for your planning team to collect their guidance for your next planning steps by asking:
- Are we comfortable using our asset in this way? How might we mitigate risks?
- Are we open to long-term contracts with the envisioned partners?
- If the museum needs to invest capital, what is the minimum return on investment (ROI) we should seek?
- Where do we get the expertise to do this effectively?
- How confidential or transparent should we be now?
- What is the approval process and public announcement sequence?

5. *Make the deal*

This crucial step is best defined at your end. This step takes the leading candidate from proposals with detailed descriptions to discussions with potential partners to written agreements to proceed, pending board approval. At this point you have a fish on the line; now it is about reeling it in and landing it.

6. *Board approval*

Before presenting a final contract for board approval, remind them of their guidance in the two previous sessions and describe how the negotiated contract addresses that guidance. Then ask them to green-light the implementation by signing the contract.

7. *Implementation*

This step is also best defined at your end. The process of getting from the approved idea to an operational revenue stream may be just as described in your proposal but is likely to face external challenges, such as raising capital, getting permits, and signing on additional partners. If there are many of these, schedules may need to be extended and project off-ramps defined.

This process is about achieving the conditions specified in the contract for the first payment on the revenue start date.

POTENTIAL RESISTANCE

Significant developments can meet fierce headwinds of resistance. A project that will be good for you may be seen as bad for others; the trick is to shape and reshape the project so that it is good for all. The role of the developer—your museum in this case—is to collaborate with objectors to negotiate compromises or, failing that, to mothball the development until the conditions are better. Here are some of the sources of legitimate concern I have run across:

- Abutters and neighbors might object to added congestion, noise, incompatible activities, view obstructions, dangers to their children, and other fears.
- Competitors might object to the museum's unfair use of its public assets and non-profit status to hurt local businesses.
- Communities of interest might object to potential negative impacts on their constituents.
- Staff might object to distractions from their jobs and threats to the museum's mission and principles.
- Leadership might object to project changes after the board's approval.
- Partners and stakeholders might object to erosions of their existing arrangements and conflicts with the new proposed partners.

- Government: Codes might require the project to obtain one or more permits, each of which involves documentation of plans and compliance with local codes. Large or high-impact projects can require environmental impact studies. The permits may cost money and require professional fees.
- Government: Tax authorities may expect the project to pay sales and unrelated business income taxes.

INCREASED IMPACTS AND BENEFITS

My suggestions in this chapter aim to help you harvest more benefits from your existing assets. If none of the candidate development projects promise more benefit than their cost, then move on. But if the benefits are compelling, compatible, defensible, and achievable, then your museum has every right and possibly a duty to realize the full public benefit potential of your assets.

NOTES

1. https://www.emilydickinsonmuseum.org/exciting-news-from-the-museum/, accessed April 6, 2022.

2. In personal conversation with CEO Deborah Spiegelman c. 2012.

3. https://www.maryhillmuseum.org/News_Releases/2009press/2009_0128.html, downloaded April 6, 2022.

4. https://www.facebook.com/nysci/posts/10156619576183775/, downloaded April 6, 2022.

Part V
REPOSITION YOUR PROGRAMMING

You may be proud of your collections and galleries, but it is what you do with those resources that engages your audiences. Programming is what you do with your resources, yet a museum's annual program is often a lower priority than work on permanent exhibits and collections. Who programs your museum?

Select Your Creative Talents Effectively

If you actively update your museum, then you likely have an architectural, exhibit, or media project in the pipeline that your team has been planning. Now it is finally funded. Time to select the outside talents you need to complement your in-house team. The strength and nature of your in-house team, including long-term advisors, are essential to selecting outside talent. The objectives of this larger team are to realize your desired outcomes within your museum's guiding principles. You may also have a vision of how this project will break new ground, set higher standards, inspire people, and draw crowds.

Which selection process will be most effective at achieving your objectives? Said another way, how do you choose with whom you'll have creative relationships?

Often, the process of selection is just right for finding the best talents to help a museum realize its objectives, but I have run across too many other instances when external factors and purchasing policies forced selection methods that compromised the project—low bids that shorted the scope, team fights, misunderstandings, untested ideas, or bad chemistry and follow-through. This chapter allows me to air the problems and suggest solutions.

I suggest that when your business model depends on producing effective and attractive programming (see chapter 6), then each project's objectives and your museum's guiding principles should drive talent selection policy.

If you agree, your museum and the scores of independent contractors who provide museums with creative services may start shifting over to the selection models used in the film, music, publishing, theater, dance, opera, and other creative sectors. Meanwhile, many museums are stuck with models used by government agencies and corporate purchasing departments. I suggest museums that are in the creative sector should engage creative talents, as do many other creative sectors more personally and less competitively. In parallel, museums will also need to shift toward structuring the project or work environment so that contracted talents are supported and encouraged to do new work while still being compelled to produce.

The main difference is that these other creative sectors hire individuals, while museum capital projects often hire companies or, even worse, teams of companies, with whoever happens to work for them assigned to your project.

If your museum produces the exhibits and programs you present, then this chapter may be useful as a way to rethink how you select the creative talents you need to complement your in-house staff.

START BY CLARIFYING WHAT YOU WANT

What kind of creative talents do you seek for your next project? It helps to start a selection process by defining not just the skills and talents you want but the level: Are you looking for a leader or a team player? Broad-brush conceptualizer or fine detailer? Visionary artist or solution designer? You may want all of these serving different functions as properly managed by your team.

Recognize that at the start, you only think you know what you want. If the desired scope is truly creative, you should be flexible to adapt and adopt new ideas.

All museum professions can have creative aspects, but exhibit developer Joe Ansel talks about a museum's business relationships for scopes of work that entail creative work in at least three categories:

- The creative work of an individual artist selected because of their past body of work and their name—you can't commission a Jeff Koons sculpture from someone else.
- Art, designs, or inventions that are new enough, or project specific enough, that they cannot be easily specified. An example of this sort of scope might be: "We need an engaging centerpiece for our atrium that should be visually compelling, resonate clearly with our mission and existing or planned content, be reasonably easy to maintain, and cost less than $500,000."
- Work that has at least one and perhaps many creative elements but can be more easily specified and for which there are clear professional standards. Examples are label writing, architectural work, and architectural and product photography.

Are you after a fixed-cost, fixed-scope agreement, or are you open to work on an hourly basis, allowing the scope to evolve? Hourly arrangements with a not-to-exceed upper limit are the worst from the contractor's view but the best from the museum's. I favor fair contracts over contracts highly favorable to one side. For instance, for a small job, a simple hourly agreement for monthly billing allows the museum to compare the total to the project completion status and budget. If progress billings get out of line, then you can make mutual adjustments in scope and expectations.

Do you seek teams or team members? Most museum projects I have been involved with called for creative teams more than solo artists. Architecture, exhibits, and media are usually collaborative arts, engaging complementary talents to cocreate the end result. Keith Sawyer's work researching team creativity finds that trust and respect among the teammates are key to group creativity. How do you establish that trust? Do you hire the team as a whole as you might an architectural and engineering firm? Or do you hire individuals to join your team as you might combine a local designer with a guest curator?

Who owns the project? And who has the vision for it? Are they the same person? If not, then how strong is their relationship? Or is the project a blank slate waiting for someone to create the vision? Staff exhibit and program professionals may have different visions than the creative talents they hire, causing personal tensions. What dynamics describe the relationships you want among your project's talents?

Lastly, and perhaps most importantly, how do you select talents who share your museum's guiding principles? Does a potential contractor share the museum's commitment to diversity and sustainability? To accuracy and documentation? Are they honest in their work, relationships, and billings?

Different selection models work better for different kinds of creative talents, so knowing the role you expect to fill should precede choosing your selection model.

SELECTION MODELS

There are many ways museums select creative talent. At the end of his long tour with patron Alice Walton of the wooded site that would become Crystal Bridges Museum of American Art (Bentonville, Arkansas), the architect Moshe Safdie asked her, "How will you select your architect?" Ms. Walton replied, "I just did." That quick, intuitive choice resulted in a spectacular merger of mission, money, architecture, and nature, but I have many more stories when poorly made choices resulted in poorly made results.

The effectiveness of a creative project depends on making the right talent choices the right ways. Assuming you are not going to hire designers, artists, or other creatives as museum employees for the project's term—an in-house option that has its own pros and cons—this chapter suggests three selection models to help you find the right fit for your needs and project. Feel free to mix and match; there are many variants and steps between these three models, which range from narrow to wide in their selection size:

- Sole source
- Interview and portfolio review
- Request for proposals (RFPs)

I've been both client and contractor using all three selection models, and I've lived with the results.

At the simplest, low-dollar level, most museums have files of regular independent contractors they rehire as needed without a lot of red tape. Label writers, public relations specialists, photographers, conservators, graphic designers, researchers, human resources consultants, evaluators, program presenters, and other individual contractors extend and complement staff.

But when the dollars get serious, the project will be highly visible, or public money is involved, then selection processes can get complicated. In museum capital projects for building expansions, renovations of old wings or new exhibitions, RFPs are too often the answer because only a few museums are funded and run by a single, decisive Ms. Walton. If sole source is the simplest selection process and RFPs the most complicated, then portfolio interviews lie in between and are often my preference.

This chapter explores three alternative ways to select creative talents for large creative projects. Choosing them by your objectives and guiding principles rather than by external pressures should increase the effectiveness of your facilities and exhibitions. Changing how you select talent should evolve gradually because staff capacities need to develop project management skills as well. Before getting to the three models, I'll describe the recent problems to clarify the need for shifting how museums select their talents.

THE PROBLEMS WITH THE CURRENT SUPPLY CHAIN FOR CREATIVE SERVICES

Before the lockdowns of 2020 and 2021, aisle after aisle of expensive trade show booths filled the MuseumExpo at the American Alliance of Museums (AAM's), annual conferences. Sales forces flew in on flush expense accounts. Slick displays in big city convention centers showcased exhibit firms, architects, traveling exhibition distributors, media suppliers, and other museum service firms living off museum revenues. Typically, 260 exhibitors and 5,000 attendees traveled to just one of the many annual conferences of a $16 billion museum industry that attracted 850 million visits annually.[1]

Many of these booths, particularly the creative services, were led by big names touted as visionaries, usually white males. While their sales force burnished their bosses' legends, the big names were seldom in the booth. This often turned out to be true during the work.

Museum operating budgets are relatively tight and closely guarded by department managers, but the money lies in museum capital budgets. Once they are funded by combinations of public and private funds in the millions, the resulting capital projects—a new wing, or gallery renovation, or new theater system, or renewed visitor center—are often rushed, expensive, and loosely managed by disconnected folks often unfamiliar with such projects professionally. New interactive exhibits can run $500 per net square foot and more if digital programming is involved. The starchitect buildings that house them might cost an additional $1,000 per gross square foot. Museum capital projects can create feeding frenzies among museum service providers, who join bidding teams competing for multimillion-dollar contracts.

I find this system both wasteful and deceptive. As museums recover from the economic damage of the pandemic, the field should rethink how much it pays for exhibits, programs, and renovations and to whom. It needs to cost less to stay fresh. The current structure adds layers of expense and uncertainty between you and whomever gets assigned to do your project.

For me, another foundational problem with museum exhibitions is that I find most of them pleasant but unstimulating. The few great exhibitions I've experienced are the enemy of the good because they show me how transformative they can be when the creative talents are aligned and supported, like a great play, concert, or movie. Among the powerful, inspirational exhibitions that reshaped my thinking and outlook are the Rothko Chapel (Houston, Texas), Gunther von Hagens's *Body Worlds*, *Teen Tokyo* by the Boston Children's Museum, Judy Chicago's *Dinner Party*, the Science Museum of Minnesota's *RACE: Are we so different?*, *T.C. Cannon: At the Edge of America*, and many of the other recent exhibitions at the Peabody Essex Museum (PEM; Salem, Massachusetts). PEM has the grace to credit the individuals on the large teams (staff and independent contractors) who create their immersive, multisensory, multidisciplinary visitor experiences. We need more such excellent museum engagements.

I suggest reducing dependence on big-ticket RFPs and increasing the use of the other two selection models: sole source and portfolio interviews. For this to work, museum staff need enough project management experience to select and manage good vendors, and there must be continuity of management from the beginning to completion.

SOLE SOURCE SELECTION

Sole source is the simplest model for selecting a contractor. You decide who should get the gig without a formal process, though you should ask colleagues about their experience with the contractor. A sole source contractor can be selected with a phone call or email. It is most frequently used when you already know the contractor, the task is clear to both of you, and when the dollars are small or the time is tight. It is also justified when the designated contractor already is contracted with the museum, familiar with your ways, or uniquely qualified to do the job (i.e., no one else can handle the scope) or when you're commissioning an artist because of their past work and reputation. On a creative team basis, sole source contracts become the continuing foundation of your long-term relationships with key outside creative talents such as label writers, sound mixers, graphic artists, textile restorers, and so on.

I find museum managers list many criteria for selecting such individual contractors. Skill, experience, reasonable fees, and local availability are prerequisites. But there are many photographers out there; how do you choose one? Your workload and aspirations get involved in the selection. The path of least resistance, least risk, and best outcomes favors selecting those talents who already know and understand the museum, are proven to be great at what they do, have good chemistry with staff, and are totally trustworthy—your regulars.

Sounds nice, doesn't it? An arrangement for expanding your staff when you have both a need and the budget for it.

Pros: You can contract with professionals you have worked with before and can trust to understand, follow, and deliver for you. The contractor must be interested, available, and affordable before you will select them as a sole source. Sole source selections take little time and they can get working right away. You may be nurturing a creative team.

Cons: By definition, you are playing favorites. You are selecting the person or firm that you already favor for the job before opening the search to others. You miss the opportunity to refresh your pool of talents. You may be enabling an old-boy network of cronies, but at best you may have reasonably low-cost, skilled help at hand with just a phone call or email.

INTERVIEWS AND PORTFOLIOS REVIEWS

Interviews and portfolio reviews invite live presentations to a selection committee by three to six potential contractors. In advance, you send them a loosely defined scope and interview questions. Their presentations typically sequence the candidates' credentials in a slide show, with their response to the museum's scope and questions, and followed by an open discussion to explore their team's interactions with yours. In addition to the presentation and interviews, committee members might visit the contractor in their workshop or studio and visit places where their past work can be seen. Perhaps you invite two or three of them back for a second round, which might include joint brainstorming to see how collaboration might work between the two teams. Gathering all selection committee members for all interviews is a challenge, because missing one results in an unfair vote. The committee should meet soon after to compare notes and either make a final choice or issue a set of clarification questions. A final meeting of the committee makes the decision, and your project manager phones the winner, pending contract negotiation.

If you can meet with a few potential designers a few times to get to know them—what a colleague calls "falling in love"—then the choice to contract with them becomes a continuation of a relationship already in progress.

Pros: Selecting creative talents by personal interview and examining their work spaces and past work is a more telling way to assess their passion for the work and their compatibility and chemistry with your team. It is also the way other creative arts often select their talents. Feature films and legit theaters select qualified individuals through casting calls, screen tests, and portfolio reviews. These are forms of interview selections.

Cons: Because of meeting limitations, you cannot invite all interested firms but must start with a short list, all too often including "the usual suspects" with maybe one or two fresh faces. Without foresight, this selection model can have loose cannons later in contracting, unless the written scope, fee, schedule, and business terms are established before the winner is announced.

When the person you will be working with and their specific talents, drive, and attitude are important to your museum project, I recommend using the interview process over competitive, impersonal RFPs. But when the project is complex, requiring the coordination of many players, I recommend using competitive RFPs.

REQUESTS FOR PROPOSALS

Requests for proposals (RFPs) invite potential contractors to submit their proposed *scope, schedule,* and *fee,* along with their credentials and references, in competition with others. Usually, the client—your museum, for instance—issues the RFP that describes the project and the desired scope of work for the winning bidder. RFPs can also include the budget, timetable, selection criteria, and other helpful information.

RFPs take many forms. The simplest is a phone call or email to a handful of known potential contractors asking them to submit proposals for a described task. The most complicated I have seen, for the design and build of a new museum's exhibits, included the components listed in table 10.1.

Prime contractors assemble teams of firms ("subs") to respond to RFPs with multidisciplinary scopes. When the authorities in a large US city issued the RFP for a new museum, they asked for everything they thought was needed to design the large, landmark museum. We were on Zaha Hadid Architect's team as the museum planners, brought on by colleagues who were to handle the exhibit design scopes. The proposed team included engineers, equipment specialists, cost estimators, and other subs needed to fill out the scope. Few of us had worked together before; each of us may have had a different approach, and each of us had to promise to deliver for a fixed cost by a fixed date. Although we were also on many winning teams, both as primes and subs, we were fortunate that bid went to another star architect.

I find RFPs that include design competitions can create long-term problems greater than their short-term benefits. When a museum asks a short list of architects or exhibit designers to submit their proposed designs in competition with others, the museum can get an array of pretty pictures, a winner to announce to the media, and a head

Table 10.1. Request for Proposals (RFP): Full List

1. Form a voluntary selection committee with board and staff members, plus key stakeholders. Send a preliminary draft of the project description and desired scope.
   a. Meet to discuss project and rank selection criteria.
   b. Identify staff or consultant support.

2. List of potential bidders sent to committee and other advisors for additions, resulting in the long list.

3. Description of project and desired scope, budget, and schedule sent to committee and legal review.
   a. Ranked selection criteria, with scorecards.
   b. Ratify attachments, such as drawings, plans, research, etc.

4. Request for qualifications (RFQ) sent to long list of bidders with a simple summary description inviting letters of interest in bidding if short-listed.
   a. Post on public and professional sites to qualify as an open bid process.

5. Selection committee reviews letters of interest and the credentials according to the criteria scorecard and narrows the field to the short-listed bidders.
   a. Short-listed bidders notified and given the bid due date and interview dates.
   b. Unlisted bidders thanked.

6. Final, full RFP and its attachments and stipulations reviewed by committee and legal counsel (the RFP becomes an attachment to the eventual contract).
   a. Updated orientation attachment includes project purpose, description, and key considerations and dates.
   b. All business terms to be in the final contract revealed so bidder can price accordingly or list exceptions in their proposal.

7. RFP sent to the short-listed bidders.

8. On-site tour and orientation for bidders, with first Q&A session.

9. Q&A period for bidders to submit written questions.
   a. Draft answers to questions and review draft with committee.

10. Client sends written answers at the same time to all the questions to all the bidders.

11. Proposal due date.

12. Received proposals tallied, checked for compliance with prerequisite criteria.
    a. Qualifying proposals sent to selection committee.

13. Committee members read proposals, fill in preliminary scorecard.

14. Selection committee meets to discuss proposals.
    a. Clarification questions (if any) sent to each proposer.

15. Clarification answers due date; sent to committee.

16. Selection committee meets again to select two to four finalists: final scorecard.
    a. Finalists notified and given interview dates.
    b. Non-finalists thanked.

17. Interview questions developed and sent to finalists.

18. Live interviews with the selection committee.

19. Selection committee meets to select winning proposer.
    a. Winner notified.
    b. Letter of Intent to Contract sent to winner.
    c. Any contract issues resolved. The RFP should include the actual contract text, or you may find your low bidder backing out of the deal once they see the contract.

20. Winner issues a work plan, detailing workshop and delivery dates.
    a. Thank-you letters sent to all participants.
21. Sign formal contract, issue notice to proceed, and first payment.
    a. Contract start date.
22. Media release announcing the museum's choice.

start on a design solution for free or little money. But because the firms can't dialogue with your team to fully understand your needs, a jury-pleasing design can carry later operational, cost, permitting, and logistical problems, such as poor layouts, too much glass, or an expensive computer simulation.

Fairness, likely among your museum's guiding principles already in some form, should rule RFP competitions. Favoring one bidder over another not only violates ethical standards but also may expose the museum to liability for damages to the other bidders. Fairness means every bidder should receive the same information at the same time, meet the same deadlines, be judged by the same criteria, and by committee members who have attended all presentations. Bidders prize inside information they can use to better target their proposal, and they will call staff to ask questions. We imposed a "cone of silence" during major bids, asking staff to route all questions through one official liaison. That staff member collected the questions but did not answer them directly. Instead, the museum posted its answers, along with the questions, to all bidders at the same time (see steps 8–10 and 14–15 in table 10.1).

I feel strongly that museums should have the funding in place before requesting formal proposals, particularly if they are calling for design submissions. Bidders invest many hours responding to RFPs and design competitions, and it is infuriating to win, yet find there is no prize. I have run across museums fishing for free fundraising props to raise money for their project. This may be alright if admitted up front (many bidders will back out), or if the museum partners with a vendor to co-sell a project, with the vendor certain to do the work once funded.

Pros: Using the RFP process to select a contractor can be justified when the client lacks the capacity to coordinate the project, the scale and potential liabilities of the project demand firms rather than individuals, the scope can be clearly defined, one of the funding sources stipulates an open bidding process, or a public spotlight is on the selection process. RFPs are also useful when you want to get inspired by new ideas and talents, provided you award the bid to one of the responders.

Open bids can introduce new talents to the museum if the RFP is widely announced. The open, fair competition allows individuals and firms who want to work with you to approach you on equal footing to firms established in your sector. Even if their credentials cannot compete with the established firms on this RFP, you may remember them when selecting your next sole source or interview talents. The museum needs to balance seasoned professionals with new talent, and some of your selection methods should help the museum stay fresh.

RFPs are a way to commit the lowest bid to your terms. If you want to find out who will do some version of the scope for the least amount of money, including firms who may be underbidding to survive or to enter a new field or in ignorance of the true costs, then a competitive bid may identify a low bidder. But is saving money more important than other project objectives?

RFPs excel at delegating complicated, multifirm projects to prime contractors who then take on the project management, assuring the museum of full coverage ("nothing falling through the cracks"). Architecture and engineering (A&E) teams can respond to RFPs seeking complete design services for a new wing or renovation. The team might include six to twelve specialized firms, but the museum can look to the prime contractor to coordinate all their work into a code-compliant set of construction documents. RFPs are a proven way to specify responsibilities and liabilities on fixed-cost, fixed-scope projects.

Cons: Yet there are other situations where using the RFP process can compromise your museum's goals when the scope is creative and somewhat open-ended, you seek individual talents, you want the contractor to work within your team, you can't define the desired outcomes because you want truly new outcomes, you can't specify the product because you want the artist or visionary designer to create it, you are in a hurry, you don't have the resources to conduct a fair RFP, or you need assurance that the work will be done well. RFPs can waste months when you already know what you want and who you want to do it.

Moreover, if the low bidder is truly ignorant of the real cost or what you want created, accepting a low bid may lead to substandard goods or, in the case of the collapse of a major vendor, no goods at all. Some large firms will sign adverse contracts because they have lawyers and legal ploys that allow them to transform their low bid into a much higher cost via change orders and other strategies.

Successful firms—some of which might well do the best work—will simply refuse to submit a proposal. They may have work and don't need your work, will not agree to your terms, know you may be fishing for ideas, or suspect you have a favorite and that they would be a straw dog in the bidding. If you are looking for creative work, few successful artists will agree to terms that make it difficult for them to control the creation and installation of their artwork. They will, for instance, want to use their own subcontractors and may have problems working on union worksites.

SELECT THE RIGHT SELECTION MODEL

I have reviewed the three selection models to remind you of some possible ways to choose talents. Ideally, you decided on some version of these models that you think is best for your project after considering the pros and cons summarized in table 10.2.

Table 10.2. Comparison of Talent Selection Models

Typical range	Sole Source	Portfolio Interviews	Requests for Proposals (RFP)
Number considered	1	4–6	RFQ: Many RFP: 8–12
Scope definition	Varies	Loosely defined in advance	Should be as clearly defined as possible
Fairness and access	Low	Medium	High (or can create the appearance of being fair)
Length of process	Quick if you already know the vendor and their capabilities	3–4 weeks	8–14 weeks
Effort by the museum	Low	Moderate	Very high
Risk of poor choice or no qualified bidders	Medium	Low	High
Control of project by the museum	High	Good	Lower

Often, however, other factors demand priority. Perhaps you face a deadline, so you use sole source rather than take the time to consider other talents. Or you have funding that demands an RFP, though you know who would do the best job. Or your choice is not on the museum's list of approved contractors.

This chapter aims to help you plead for the project's goals as long as you stay within the museum's guiding principles. Once you know what kind of talents you seek and how they will best achieve the project's goals, then you can define a selection and contracting process and make the case for approval.

Generic purchasing policies can make selecting contractors impersonal, leading to selections of companies based on scores and numbers. This is right for buying stationary supplies and internet services but may get in the way of selecting individuals and teams where the interpersonal relationships are critical to effective museum creative projects.

I don't think the museum field will ever shift entirely to selecting individual talents as do the theater, film, and magazine fields, but the time may be right to shift the balance away from large design firms. It is less expensive to hire experienced individual talents than firms with their layers of staff and overhead, and you are sure to work with the individuals you are selecting.

POTENTIAL RESISTANCE

If your museum has purchasing policies, do they align with the museum's guiding principles and support your project's objectives? Larger and older museums tend to have policies setting out the museum's business terms and governing selection processes; these policies can result in preapproved forms for purchase orders, personal service contracts, and contractor agreements.

Of course you must work within these policies, but if they differ from the selection process you think is best for your project, consider either appealing the policy for an exception or working with management to revise the policy to better align to the museum's ongoing needs for selecting creative talents.

Open bids are a way to seek more diversity in the museum's talents, especially if the bid criteria favor minority-owned firms. However, I have found enough instances of bid teams gaming this system by including minority-owned firms in minor positions, leaving the main shares of the budget to the established firms. I prefer first diversifying the selection committee and staff (see chapter 5) and then trusting them to select the most effective creative talents given the project objectives and the museum's guiding principles. Hollywood is diversifying its talent pools because of public pressure, box office goals, and a new generation of Black and women directors, so there are other methods of broadening participation in museum creative teams than open bids.

Resistance is likely from the large design firms who win the large contracts. They may defend the high cost of museum additions and exhibits as what "museum quality" actually costs. Their firm may boast more credits than a museum might find in an individual designer, but the individuals working for the firm may have fewer credits than an experienced freelancer. They may also remind their museum clients of the needs and risks of coordinating multiple design specialties, which some museums prefer and can afford to outsource. This resistance will be motivated by maintaining their employees and overhead, including sales and management costs, distinct from their creative services.

INCREASED IMPACTS AND BENEFITS

What I am really after in this chapter is to pave the way for the magic that happens when creative talents trust each other, know each other's work, and long to work together on a project. The creative partnership among Hal Prince, Stephen Sondheim, and their regulars vitalized Broadway. Producer/director John and Roy Boulting established British humor with regulars Peter Sellers, Terry-Thomas, and Ian Carmichael. In our own field at the United States Holocaust Memorial Museum (Washington, DC), the creative collaboration between architect James Ingo Freed and exhibition designer Ralph Appelbaum resulted in one of the most powerful visitor experiences I've had. All these depended on close personal relationships among the creative talents.

STEPS TO ADAPT THE IDEAS TO YOUR MUSEUM

Start with the big picture: What are your museum's needs for creative talents? Do you need them regularly for a variety of projects or only occasionally? Which talents

DEFINITIONS 10.1

CONTRACT ATTACHMENTS

Written agreements articulate shared understandings. The principals involved should work through each contract term, with legal advice. Regardless of how you select creative talents, writing up what your contractors are doing (the scope), what they will be paid (the fees and expenses), by when (the schedule), by what rules (the business terms), and in what context (the orientation materials) paves the way for a smooth relationship. Without working all this out in advance, you are likely to run into serious misunderstanding deep into the project: Who owns the work? What deliverables are due when? What happens when it goes over budget? When is the job done?

A project's specifics tend to be in the attachments to a core contract so that these can be updated when changes are made.

Scope describes the work to be done by the contractor and can range from the general—"design an excellent visitor experience that fulfills the objectives," to the specific deliverables—"submit scaled construction drawings."

Orientation materials are a folder of project-relevant information summarizing your museum's thinking to date about the project. The folder might include the museum's conceptual framework, publicity materials, project purposes and objectives, written conceptual descriptions of the project, evaluation and research findings, floorplans, budgets, photographs of objects and spaces involved, team contact list, overall schedule, and other documents reflecting your aspirations and given conditions. A shorter version of this folder should be included in the RFP, with the full folder given to the winning bidder.

Schedule is the sequence of calendar dates or number of work weeks for each of the phases of the project, starting with the date of the notice to proceed as the official start date, and the completion date as the target end date—though many projects go later due to loose ends on the *punch list*. Completion date can be a fixed date, but more often is defined as the date the museum formally accepts the work.

Term is the period of time covered by the contract.

Fees and Expenses, also called the *payment schedule*, lists the total compensation and reimbursement that the museum intends to pay the

(continued)

DEFINITIONS 10.1 *(continued)*

contractor, provided progress and quality benchmarks have been met. Payments are often tied to acceptance of major deliverables. The first payment is due often on submission of the contractor's acceptable work plan; the last payment (the *holdback*) is sometimes scheduled after official completion to allow for warranty enforcement.

Business terms govern how the job is done. Clauses typically include definitions of terms, insurance, confidentiality, ownership of ideas and materials, termination, liability, severability, indemnification, change orders, training and support, documentation, taxes, permits and fees, damages, warrants and exclusions, quality and workmanship, warranty, access to site, delays, resolution of disagreements, code compliance, time primacy, acts of nature, notices and certificates, applicable laws, liaison officers, and other legal and procedural aspects.

should be in-house staff and which contracted as needed? Do you produce enough programs annually to set up production processes and a cadre of known contractors? Does your museum want its creative projects to reflect the look and feel of the museum's brand? Has your museum found its "voice" for its programming? Is there a potential aftermarket for your projects? (See chapter 9.)

With answers to these questions, you can talk about the scale of the issue and then suggest selection policies to increase the effectiveness of the museum's creative projects.

Then, if all goes well with implementing the suggestions in this chapters, you'll have fewer ho-hum exhibits and programs and more inspirational, transformative, and memorable museum experiences.

NOTE

1. Cited from https://blooloop.com/museum/in-depth/aam-annual-meeting-museum-expo/, accessed December 17, 2021.

11

Support New Strategies for Changing Programming

Community museums feel the pressure to change more than tourist and destination museums because repeat visits from a residential audience drive their success. Among community museums, art museums, zoos, and botanical gardens have unique ways to change content economically and frequently; respectively, they can hang different art, birth new animals, and cycle seasonally.

However, I find that most other community museums want to change and update their on-site public offerings more frequently than they can. They aspire to replace dated content and stay relevant to their community's evolving needs and aspirations, but the pace is glacial and the costs chilling. Exhibits, collections, classes, workshops, and media—what I'll call the museum's *programs*—are often in slower rotation than desired; usually lack of resources is cited as the cause.

The Peabody Essex Museum (PEM; Salem, Massachusetts) does an excellent job of programming. PEM is in the next town over from our home, and we go there frequently because either there is something new we want to see or just because we're up for wandering a museum where we know we will always see something fresh. In addition to its thirteen ongoing exhibitions, PEM typically offers the public seven temporary exhibitions a season, multiple tours, events, member gatherings, and community festivals. But then, PEM has many galleries and program spaces, a huge collection, a staff of more than two hundred experienced professionals and an endowment of more than $400 million.

How can the rest of the community museums in the United States achieve this level of active programming without these resources?

Chapter 6 suggests organizing a museum to produce and operate programs. Chapter 7 suggests setting specifications to facilitate sharing programs among museums, and chapter 8 describes the delta model of change. In this chapter I build on these ideas to propose two programming strategies: an *annual program demand calendar*, an active yearly schedule driven by demand, and a *program partnership template*, a content- and format-agnostic template to help museums define effective partnerships to produce shared programs. These ideas are followed by the likely resistance to the ideas, countered by the increased benefits and effectiveness.

Imagine a future where your museum installs new programs from your museum partners as routinely and economically as newspapers select articles from AP, UPI, and other newspapers, as public libraries borrow books from regional collections, as performing arts centers stage new shows, and as retail chains hang crates of seasonal decorations.

NEED FOR FASTER, CHEAPER, AND MORE ATTRACTIVE WAYS TO CHANGE

But first, why do community museums need to change their programming? Why more frequently? Why change more of the museum offerings?

I can hear museum managers dismiss the need with "We can't fill the programs we have; why add more?" or "We lose money on programs; why add more?"

The answers, easier said than done, are more appealing and more profitable programs, all strategically scheduled. The strategies in this chapter have those aspirations, but still, why bother changing at all?

Relevance is the clearest answer. What is appealingly relevant today is seldom as relevant a year or even a few months later. To be relevant carries an obligation to change programming.

Audiences also pressure museums to change. "What's new? Why should I come back?" Market research asking visitors why they come to a museum and why they come back finds that changing exhibitions are effective attractors. For mature *community museums*, defined as continuously serving a stable market, typically area residents rather than tourists, changing exhibitions are more effective motivators of repeat visits than a museum's permanent exhibits, though both work together.

How much of the museum's public spaces need to change to motivate repeat visits? Heureka (Vantaa, Finland) set a goal to renew at least 50 percent of its exhibition floor every year, but I have found few American museums can keep up this pace. Perception and dwell time may be more important than setting exact square footage goals. Seeing different experiences on entering a museum sets up the perception of vitality and change. Visitor dwell time in museums caps out after about ninety minutes, when museum fatigue sets in for many casual visitors, so the question is, what share of a repeat visitor's time in the galleries should be new to them? I'd argue for at least half the dwell time, if not two-thirds.

But exhibitions are not the only programs, and other program formats may be easier to change. The lockdowns during the pandemic drove innovations in digital programming, with many fast-response, bootstrap virtual programs launched quickly to reach new audiences in new ways. Now that the public is returning to museums,

CHANGING PROGRAMMING

Program (noun) is used in this book as an umbrella term embracing all museum offerings. It includes exhibits, exhibitions, collection displays, shows, public and youth programs, outreach, private and public events, services, tours, films, camp-ins, preschool/day-care sessions, presentations, concerts, meetings, festivals, parties, conferences, conservation projects, collection access, and many more. Even the core visitor experience of the permanent museum galleries is a program.[1]

To Program, Programming (verb, gerund) is the critical and creative management act of assigning specific programs to a museum's public platforms and calendar times. To program a space or a venue is to decide what programs will happen there and when. To program the museum for a year (i.e., programming all its platforms for all the year's time slots) is, in effect, to activate the museum's business plan, annual budget, thematic emphasis, and desired impacts and benefits.

Many museum professionals use *programs* to refer to a museum's *scheduled programs* as distinct from its installed exhibits and as facilitated events that happen among the exhibits and in labs, workshops, studios, and other *program spaces*, which are distinct from galleries in that they have doors which can be closed to house the *program participants*. I admit I use *program* both as an umbrella term and as this subset, depending on context to clarify each use.

Peer programmers are other producing museums with similar needs for programs.

Marketable change is a large or significant enough program change to merit investing marketing resources to promote the new program as a reason to return to the museum.

An *exhibition* is a program consisting of a group of exhibits addressing a theme or topic and integrated aesthetically into a visitor experience.

Changing exhibitions are also known as temporary exhibitions, traveling exhibitions, retrospectives, films, presentations, scenarios, shows, feature exhibitions, biennales, travelers, and installations.

An *experience platform* is a museum space (real or virtual) outfitted with infrastructure to facilitate program change through the installation of compatible scenarios. A simple example of an experience platform is a movie theater with seats, a screen, and a projector; the movies (i.e., the scenarios) change frequently at little cost, but the experience platform evolves slowly.

A *scenario* is a program that can be installed on an experience platform for a period of time, provided both are compatible in format; that is, the movie must be in a format that can be downloaded to the projector and played back over the system.

---

1. For a more complete list of potential programs, see sections 68–72 of *The Museum Manager's Compendium.*

wouldn't it be great to get that same spirit and energy into innovations in all the museum's on-site, off-site, and virtual program offerings?

YEARLY PROGRAMMING STRATEGY

The following management research questions may inform programming strategy by first exploring when your potential audiences are available and in the market for your program categories. The questions focus on the demand side:

- List your key audience segments and your program formats in a matrix. Which segments might find which formats appealing?
- Use room scheduling software to set up a daily calendar for each space/venue with roll-ups by zone and category and the ability to see a museum-wide schedule for any date range, especially the full fiscal year. Enter all the preexisting bookings and commitments, including usual heavy demands on certain spaces at certain times (e.g., student lunchroom 11:00–1:30 during the spring weekdays). How much blank space is open for programming and when?
- What are your **yearly** programming strategies with regard to:
  - In what weeks are which audiences available and likely to come?
  - When can the museum communicate to each audience most effectively?
  - What are the best windows to launch and run changing exhibitions? New learning programs? New theater shows? Lecture series? Holiday parties?
  - How often should which programs change?
- What are the **weekly** programming strategies suggested by which days and times each segment is available? School groups are not available on Friday evenings, but young adults are, for instance. What are the seasons of similar weeks, such as the summer vacation weeks and the high and low school group seasons? Note the normally heavy weeks, such as school vacation and Thanksgiving weeks.
- What are the **daily** programming strategies suggested by audience availability and likelihood of engaging? Teens may be available after school, while working couples only in the evenings and weekends. What independent access zones does this suggest? (See chapter 8.)

The answers to these questions allow you to plan your *yearly demand calendar* showing when each audience segment is available and likely to want to participate in your programs. Start with the clearest demands—spring school groups, Saturday classes, and so on—then move to when your audiences are available and can be motivated to engage with the museum—vacations and holidays, evening lectures, summer blockbusters, and so on. Also tint the valleys when all your audiences are focused elsewhere, such as September or January or during an election run-up.

With this demand clear, you can assign programs for the right audiences to the right times and platforms to fill in your *yearly programming calendar*.

MUSEUM PROGRAM PARTNERS

In the 1980s, the museum I worked in belonged to more than eight museum partnerships, sharing programs in many media and sizes. We were members of partnerships producing and sharing large and small traveling exhibitions, planetarium shows, robotic dinosaurs, school kits, teacher institutes, giant screen films, and more. My leader, Dr. Roger L. Nichols, was a visionary museum director who understood the value of kindred museums working together to share programs, and he was the instigator of many of these networks.

Today, most of these networks no longer exist as conceived, if at all. Some, like the Planetarium Show Network, never produced their program; some like the Museum Film Network, morphed into other purposes, but most withered away for several reasons: loss of leadership energy and faith (Dr. Nichols died in 1987); lack of a driving, profitable business model; lack of investment in compatible experience platforms; and, eventually, the fading appeal of the format or the content.

Today, with the benefit of hindsight and with visionary leadership by a few founding museums, these issues can be addressed. A template for program partnerships for different museum formats and content themes can be profitable and sustainable for the life span of a format's appeal and relevance if a critical number of museums can agree to work together.

Outside funding, such as the National Science Foundation's support of the intermuseum National Informal STEM Education Network (NISEnet) and the Institute of Museums and Library Services' early funding for the Collaboration for Ongoing Visitor Experience Studies (COVES), can help kick-start and sustain the flow of money.

Foundations and agencies like to fund partnerships among nonprofits because they can spread their money and impact to help more organizations. If your partnership is focused on school audiences or unreached publics and several museums have banded together to produce programs to serve them, then you may have a good chance to fund some or all of the venture with outside funding.

But if your idea for a program partnership is sound, and there is no outside funding available, I suggest a group of museums can run the venture themselves. It might be the cleanest and fastest way to share the production of better programs for lower per member costs.

There are already networks for producing temporary exhibitions and media programs; I am suggesting building on these to establish partnerships capable of ongoing production using amortized and shared experience platforms through a sustainable business model that benefits all parties.

I've found the business models work once six or more museums agree to partner to produce and distribute a series of programs compatible with a shared format. With each museum handling a sixth of the cost, even the additional costs of moving it around and making extra copies are affordable. Further, if each museum capitalizes a shared infrastructure experience platform and amortizes it over several scenarios, the numbers get even better. This is essentially what the science center community found with producing giant screen films through the Museum Film Network run by member museums with IMAX experience platforms. Once there was an international network of compatible experience platforms—the IMAX theaters—the marketplace boomed with high-quality films generating significant attendance for more than two decades.

Shared interests in a content theme, audience segment, and program format link the partnering museums. The museums can be peers in the same discipline or neighboring museums serving a school district or museums with related collections or regional workforce initiatives.

When multiple museums share a program series, the content and approach will benefit from feedback and evaluation in multiple markets, and those programs achieving consistent successes will benefit the creators and establish brand trust.

The problem is getting a network started. One museum needs to be the first to commit and then to actively convince other museums to join. It is a tough sell, because each museum must agree to put money up in advance, share each other's productions, align their programming schedules, and accept a level of risk that usually makes board members uncomfortable. The convening power of the lead museum is essential.

A TEMPLATE FOR PROGRAM PARTNERSHIPS

Because program partnerships are long-term, risky ventures where the layout of cash is certain, but the return of net profits and other benefits is far from certain, the potential long-term benefits have to be appealing and likely enough to merit the up-front investments and risk.

What do I mean by "enough?" I start with an annual return on investment of 25 percent, given the risk, but might settle for half that given a very safe and lengthy term. That 25 percent means that the partnership might pay off the investment after four years of operation. It may take a year for the partnership to ship usable programs, which means five years of lost opportunity for the up-front costs, so the venture must continue to benefit the founding museums for several years after to justify the risk.

This math improves significantly once more museums join the founders, and the vision for a program partnership should aspire to this larger membership by adopting broader definitions. For instance, we attracted more museums to the Ocean Film Network to produce the giant-screen film *The Living Sea* than did a later group attracted to a giant-screen film of the Mississippi River because far more museums related to the world's oceans than to a US river.

Money is likely to be a driver of new program partnerships, and, I believe, enough money must flow to make the arrangements beneficial to all participants, especially the member museums. A sustainable and flourishing partnership provides attractive cashflow back to the program producers, the distributors, the founding museums, the later museums, and even to the partnership to cover its expenses and meetings.

My model assumes each museum receives monetary value from installing the programs either in cost savings or in new revenues from a combination of its audiences and supporters. The revenue depends in part on the program format: For a temporary exhibition it might be the admissions upcharges and sponsorships; for a ceramic studio master class, the series fees; for an after-school outreach workshop, a foundation grant; for a travel program, the sales commissions; for a webinar, a foundation grant and log-in fees; and so on. The partnering museum draws on these collected fees to pay the partnership a lease payment, which the partnership distributes back to the producer and the members after covering its expenses.

I think that vital and effective program partnerships require clear agreement up front to assure the distribution of a series of programs that can be routinely installed on a compatible experience platform somewhere in each museum's on-site, off-site, or virtual spaces. That agreement might include the answers to the questions in the following *program partnership template*:

1. What is the name of the program partnership?
2. Which museums are the founding partners?
   a. What [sectors of] museums are potential additional partners?
3. Summarize the content, the format, the intended audiences, the business model, and the scale.
   a. How will the partnership benefit the partner museums? What is the theory of action?
4. What is the purpose of this program partnership?
5. What are its guiding principles?
6. How broad is the content? How is it relevant or appealing? What should be the approach to the subject matter? List some possible program topics.
7. How many founding museums are needed to start? What incentives do founders get?
8. How many more museums might join later? Under what conditions? What are their benefits and rights compared with the founders'? Is there a maximum? Is there a third category of nonmember leases?

9. What are the specifications of the shared and capitalized experience platform? Is it branded or patented? Who supplies the platform to museums? Is it exclusive or open-source?

10. What are the specifications for the program scenarios to be installed on the experience platforms? Who owns the intellectual property?

    a. Is it a closed or open specification? Can third parties use the specification to produce competing scenarios independently of the partnership?

11. What is the partnership's business model, and what are the costs and benefits to each museum?

12. How much money is each founding museum expected to pay up front for (a) its share of the production and distribution costs; (b) outfitting its own space to meet the specs for the experience platform; (c) installing and operating the program; and (d) funding the partnership's costs?

    a. How many deposits must be collected before the deposits become nonrefundable and spendable?

13. What will be the similar costs for additional members?

14. What is the schedule? When is the partnership officially funded? When will the first program be ready for distribution? When should members operate the program and for how long?

    a. What is the payment schedule and time frame for each museum's participation?

15. What is the initial frequency of new, compatible programs? How are they funded?

    a. How many programs are capitalized by the initial payments?

    b. What is the desired frequency of change? How many new programs a year?

    c. What is involved in changing programs in time, effort, and cost? How much downtime between programs?

16. How is the partnership organized and governed? Who is in charge? How will agreements be enforced?

17. How is the partnership managed and administered? What reports are shared? Who staffs it?

18. How will the partnership handle ancillary materials such as teacher packages, marketing materials, and media kits?

19. What are the provisions for off-ramps and terminations?

20. What outcome data might indicate success?

These questions may be more than a simple partnership needs but become important as the scale of the venture increases. They are not intended as an outline of a partnership agreement, however. Before that legally binding formality, they are intended to prompt discussion among potential founding museums, ideally building consensus around the partnership and its promise as the venture takes shape.

POTENTIAL RESISTANCE

Resistance to a museum-wide yearly program calendar may come from departments used to controlling a subset of the museum's spaces and program types. For instance, the education department may protect their relationship with regional teachers by wanting to negotiate times, spaces, and programs directly with school group teachers. Centralizing a process often runs against resistance from those who fear change and loss of control. As with the example of school group bookings, you may hear valid reasons to refine the process and include grandfathered provisions during a transition term.

My second suggestion for program partnerships is likely to run against greater, more substantive resistance due to issues with staffing, money, scheduling, and the relative riskiness of the idea.

I am not suggesting all a museum's programs should come from partnerships. Some share of the annual programs should be grounded in local relevance and unique to just that museum.

I find that staff limitations often explain why museums do not offer more programs. I can hear managers asking, wisely, "Who will produce, market, install, operate, and evaluate all these new programs?" Under this question may be "Why do we need to do more? We're doing all we can now."

As public assets, museums should maximize the good created by the effective use of their resources. Staff is one of a museum's resources, and if staff is maxed out, adding programs in the short term may be a nonstarter.

However, if your facility and systems are not maximized (see chapter 8), then consider adding and shifting staff in parallel with expanding programs that add revenues and serve more people.

If the staffing issue can be addressed, then I've found that money, timing, and risk are the next lines of resistance to joining program partnerships.

Many museums do not have enough discretionary money to pay their share of the up front costs, especially as the results may not pay back within that fiscal year. These initial costs are seldom in the official budget, and adding them to next year's budget delays the partnership and introduces new uncertainties. Partnership costs can appear to be outside pressures on a museum's budget, when there are usually inside staff with spending agendas of their own, which often end up taking priority. First a museum must want to invest in a partnership, and then it has to approve a budget that includes that money. Programs should be added only if their projected earned and support revenues are likely to exceed their projected costs.

Timing can be an issue because museums schedule well in advance and aligning open slots for a coordinated opening is difficult. Although many programs do not need to open at the same time, even opening within one fiscal year is challenging due to previous commitments, lockdowns, theme seasons, and public service initiatives.

These are substantive resistance issues facing the formation of new program partnerships. Success will depend on attractive ventures and strong museum leadership. It makes sense for peer museums in separate markets to share the cost of shared programs; the challenge is to get through the roadblocks.

INCREASED IMPACTS AND BENEFITS

Because relevance changes rapidly and audiences want change, so should community museums change frequently to better serve their purposes and to engage their audiences and supporters more often to build deeper and more effective relationships.

Scheduling a museum's yearly programming based on when its audiences are available is likely to increase use and efficiency during those times and save money when they are not. A yearly programming calendar can improve the fit between the museum's offerings and its audience's needs, making the museum more effective.

Cheaper and better programs should help museums achieve more frequent rates of appealing, profitable program changes. Cheaper and better are not likely outcomes for single museum productions but may become possible when the number of programs and the number of museums operating them scale up. Cheaper and better programs might happen when museums work together to make them happen.

Incremental revenue and decreased costs make a compelling argument for going forward with programming partnerships, but increased frequency of change and quality of the program could also drive the initiative.

In addition to benefiting the participating museums, program partnerships can offer sponsors and talents a larger, possibly national audience than any single museum. Once six or more museums agree to install a program, then their producer should be able to contract talent and endorsements possible only because of the larger, wider audience and revenue flow. This larger audience might also justify the use of known role models, such as Jane Goodall hosting a program on conservation or Michelle Obama hosting a program on food health. Once the audience size gets beyond the break-even point, then producers might justify larger budgets, which would increase the quality and impact of the programs they produce.

These two suggestions to form a yearly programming calendar based on demand and to form program partnerships aspire to help museums become vitally alive through more frequently changing programming within reasonable museum budgets.

Part VI
RESTORE
MANAGEMENT BASICS

We have been too dependent on the kindness of others. We often assume that our wealthy board members will make up our deficits and cover our emergencies, that it is OK not to fund depreciation, that the summer crowds will certainly pay back our endowment drawdowns, or that our mission is too well-loved to be out of sync.

We will be stronger once we are less dependent and more self-sufficient . . . more professional.

Measure, Document, and Communicate Your Impacts

Your museum probably does so much more than just foster visual literacy, connect us to our shared heritage, advance STEM learning, or increase and diffuse knowledge. It is time to tout and count all your impacts and benefits in addition to your mission outcomes.

For decades, I have been concerned about museum accountability. Museums have made great strides in performance measurement, but museums do not yet agree on ways to account for a museum's impacts. Museum administrators need measurements to prove their museum's value, to advocate for their institutions, and to improve their performance.

The hypothesis is that managing and improving a museum's desired impacts can be strengthened by choosing appropriate sources of data and comparing them to (1) a baseline situation and change over time, (2) peer museums, or (3) recognized benchmarks. A *data-informed museum* uses these data comparisons and trends to document likely changes in impact, provide new insights, identify best practices, set staff objectives, and make more effective decisions.

There are many ways proposed to evidence our impacts. The literature is full of reports, studies, and papers documenting the public value of museums, and they present compelling evidence that museums are valuable to society and individuals. But how do we measure that value using numbers that quantify change over time so that we can see if we are getting better?

One of the many challenges facing the advancement of a data-informed management culture is the museum field's lack of a centralized agency to establish shared definitions and methods of measuring, documenting, and communicating museum impacts (see chapter 7). Once museums can measure their impacts consistently year to year, compare them to peer and local museums, test out strategies, report to supporters, and arm advocates, then museums will get even better and more effective.

Until then, however, museums can still use the data they have to account for their impacts and make them more effective. In this chapter I suggest four initiatives to consider including among your other management initiatives:

- Integrate research operationally.
- Identify the categories of your desired impacts.
- Count museum engagements and not just visits.
- Select data fields to monitor your desired impacts.

But first, a review of the theory behind these initiatives.

MUSEUM THEORY

As museum sage Stephen E. Weil observed, the value of a museum lies in its contributions: What impacts did the museum achieve this year? For whom? And at what cost/value to whom? How has it changed someone's life? How has it changed its community?

Museum director John Cotton Dana wrote a century ago that museums should suit themselves to their community's needs. Museum researcher John Falk reminded us that museums are a free choice—no one has to go—and evaluator George Hein urges museums to honor their duty as public resources to make the world better and more democratic.

These conceptual foundations have implications for today's museums:

- To be useful, museums need to understand the needs and aspirations of their communities and be structured to address those needs.
- To have an impact and create public value, museums should understand that their vast resources (means) need to be deployed to achieve their purposes (ends) and be evaluated on how effectively and efficiently they do so.
- To be successful in a competitive marketplace, museums must offer experiences and services their audiences and supporters find valuable and relevant.
- To make the world better and more democratic, museums need to aspire to set examples and serve the public.

Synthesized, these concepts underlie museum economic theory: The community funds the museum to use its resources to provide effective services back to the community. The museum provides these services efficiently and, instead of privatizing its net revenues, contributes to community development and social good. People and organizations pay money, spend time, and make efforts to engage with a museum in return for the impacts and benefits they receive. The cumulative time, effort, and resources that a museum's audiences and supporters voluntarily provide in exchange for the benefits they get from the museumare some indicators of its value to its stakeholders.

Museums can use this *exchange data* to measure changes in audience engagements. The number of visits indicates cumulative effort exchanged for the museum's visitor experiences; the money they spend indicates their acceptance of a market value, and the time they dwell indicates their interest and degree of engagement. Changes in these numbers, both per program and museum-wide, can inform management actions.

This theory was tested in concept by the two-year Assessing Museum Impact (AMI) pilot research project that explored whether the use of data would help museums improve their impact (effectiveness) and performance (efficiency). Led voluntarily by five senior museum professionals (I was among the authors) and coordinated by the New England Museum Association (NEMA), the project was designed to assist six midsize New England museums to select data using the PIID Sequence (see table 12.1) and then to use that data strategically. The participants reported positive impacts on their management culture and actionable enhancements to their museums. All plan to continue using data strategically.

Building on this theory and a career analyzing museum numbers, I offer these four initiatives to help museums use data strategically to achieve your desired impacts more effectively.

IDENTIFY THE CATEGORIES OF YOUR DESIRED IMPACTS

Your museum's intentional purposes may be unique, but they are likely to fit within larger categories of museum impact and benefit. You may be focused on, say, conserving duck decoys, as is the Peoria Riverfront Museum (Peoria, Illinois), but you are also in the larger category of *preserving heritage*. You may be developing school curricula, as does the Lawrence Hall of Science (Berkeley, California), but you are also in the larger category of *serving education.*

Recognizing your membership in these larger categories of potential museum impact and benefit, listed in table 12.1, can help you identify supporters interested in your work, kindred organizations with similar goals, and guide you to data fields used by others to monitor outcomes in each category.

The categories come from my 2016 analysis of the database of 1,025 Museum Indicators of Impact and Performance ("MIIP 1.0"),[1] drawn from more than fifty museum sources globally, that revealed twelve broad areas of external impact and two of internal impact. I grouped the indicators by who they were for and who was funding the services. In this approach, the indicators fell under four impact sectors:

Public impacts benefit the public as a whole and tend to be funded by government and private philanthropy; *private impacts* tend to benefit businesses and corporations;

Table 12.1. Categories of Potential Museum Impact and Benefit

Potential Museum Impacts	Total Indicators
Public Impacts	
A. Broadening participation	85
B. Preserving heritage	47
C. Strengthening social capital	76
D. Enhancing public knowledge	43
E. Serving education	56
F. Advancing social change	40
G. Communicating public identity and image	27
Private Impacts	
H. Contributing to the economy	85
I. Delivering corporate community services	9
Personal Impacts	
J. Enabling personal growth	147
K. Offering personal respite	4
L. Welcoming personal leisure	11
Institutional Impacts	
M. Helping museum operations	308
N. Building museum capital	87
Total Indicators in the MIIP 1.0 database	**1025**

personal impacts benefit individuals, families, and groups; and *institutional impacts* benefit the museum. The impact areas are divided into seven categories of public impacts (i.e., broadening participation, preserving heritage, strengthening social capital, enhancing public knowledge, serving education, advancing social change, and communicating public identity and image); two private impacts (contributing to the economy and delivering corporate community services); three personal impacts (enabling personal growth, offering personal respite, and welcoming personal leisure); and two institutional impacts (helping museum operations and building museum capital).

These fourteen varieties of potential museum impacts and benefits embrace many subheads. *Enabling personal growth*, for instance, includes learning, identity development, inspiration, and many more ways museums help individuals grow in skills, knowledge, and esteem, and *preserving heritage* includes collection conservation, cultural identity, and access to history.

Many museum activities provide multiple services. A *Titanic* exhibition, for instance, may provide personal growth and leisure benefits to its visitors, deliver corporate community services to its sponsors, and contribute to economic impact by generating tourism.

Your museum's intentional purposes are likely to relate to multiple categories. Seeing your purposes in light of these wider categories may help identify funding sources operating in each category, other organizations with complementary purposes, and data fields others have used to monitor their outcomes. Filtering the MIIP database by your chosen impact category lists potential data fields that might measure the indicators of your desired impacts.

INTEGRATE RESEARCH OPERATIONALLY

Chapter 6 proposes a departmental organization with a separate research and evaluation office (REO) that measures outcomes and looks at the trends from operating data and surveys to inform decisions. That chapter focused on the evaluation role; this chapter looks at the data research role.

Integrating the various forms of research into one REO offers several advantages over current practice of different departments each conducting their own studies: efficiency, consistency, depth, cross-pollination, institutional memory, independent evaluation, vendor selection, and professional practices. REO can be the museum's brain, processing incoming information, packaging it for the museum's needs, and sending it out to relevant staff. REO maintains the museum's archives and its links to content and evaluation experts, as well as its data service accounts. REO handles the museum's program content, evaluation, research, and data needs centrally.

The REO is headed by the museum's chief research officer, who reports to the CEO, meaning data collection and evaluation are independent of the project teams. This arm's length independence reduces bias, enforces professional methods, and increases accuracy. The office will release regular bulletins to managers.

Germane to this chapter, REO is in charge of data collection, analysis, and reporting. The office calculates and posts the museum's key performance indicators (KPIs) by collecting data generated by operating the museum. Data could come from the admissions system, the reservations bookings, the accounting system, HR stats, exhibit interactions, and crowd sensors in the public spaces.

As part of its data reporting, the REO could manage the museum's dashboard displays, alerting managers to actionable data in their departments. As the REO would also be aware of relevant external evaluation findings and trends, the REO could make recommendations to management for improvements to performance and impact.

In addition to this cross-roughing among different kinds of research, there are other advantages to integrating the museum's research and evaluation needs. Staff can be trained researchers, and the office can house and recall all content, studies, and data. If the museum has a library, it could fit in the REO organizationally. At base, the job of managing the museum's information is assigned, centralized, and integrated.

PERFORMANCE, IMPACT, BENEFIT, AND INDICATOR

Because *key performance indicator* (KPI) is a widely used term, I use it in this book, though I make a distinction between impact and performance. Technically, I should call them key impact and performance indicators (KIPIs) and then separate KIIs from KPIs, but I won't.

The REO collects data according to the data fields needed for the KPIs. Management, possibly with board guidance, determines the museum's impact KPIs using the *PIID Sequence* (see below). *Impact* is about how effective your museum is at achieving your intentional purposes. Impact KPIs might include the number of active partnerships, publications per curator, collection share on view, new jobs created, and teacher renewal rate. *Performance* is about how efficiently your museum operates. Performance KPIs might include utility costs per square foot, marketing cost per visit, and so on. As performance indicators are already widely used, I'll focus on impact indicators in this chapter.

A museum aspires to have *impacts* on its community, audiences, and supporters. The community, audiences, and supporters receive *benefits* from the museum. The benefits can be different from the impact: A family visiting an aquarium receives the benefit of a quality family experience, while the aquarium's desired impact on the family is to heighten their awareness of conserving biodiversity. Or the benefits and impacts can be aligned: New parents bring their toddler to a children's museum to see the child develop and learn with new kinds of challenges; the children's museum's mission is child development. Studying the alignment between a museum's benefits and impacts may illuminate potentials and inefficiencies. It is useful to remember the distinction, which hinges on their prepositions: Society, individuals, and organizations receive benefits *from* the museum. The museum has impacts *on* society, individuals, and organizations. Benefits are in the eyes of the receiver; impacts are in the desires of the museum.

Potential *indicators* of a museum's impacts and benefits on others and its performance in achieving those impacts include evaluation criteria, institutional success measures, foundation objectives, management resources, proposed indicators, research findings, and data collection fields from routinely asked surveys. Indicators are either quantitative or qualitative and may indicate to some expert audience potentially meaningful data related to measuring museum impact and performance. *Indicator* is the generic, encompassing term. A mission statement is an indicator of the museum's primary purpose; its annual budget is an indicator of the scale of operations, and its visitor satisfaction levels and supporter repeat levels are indicators of its impacts on visitors and supporters, respectively.*

---

* The Museum Indicators of Impact and Performance (MIIP 1.0) is a database of 1,025 indicators drawn from fifty-one sources normalized by the White Oak Institute and available for free (search for "MIIP 1.0"). Every indicator is tagged by its category of potential impact and its step along the theory of action and the content of its data.

COUNT MUSEUM ENGAGEMENTS AND NOT JUST VISITS

Attendance counts undercount the number of museum engagements by focusing on gallery visits. I suggest counting *museum engagements* and not just gallery visits. This inclusive definition opens the museum's impact counts to more categories of public engagement with the museum, including program participants, event attendees, fundraising guests, volunteer shifts, advisory committee meetings, and the museum's other program formats on-site, outreach, and virtual. At first, you won't capture all your museum's annual public engagements, but a more comprehensive grand total and the individual program breakouts will be valuable for advocacy, accountability, and direction.

The umbrella definition of museum engagements collects a museum's many potential kinds of activities into one number across all the museum's activities. Annual *engagement counts* are an indicator of the effort the museum's beneficiaries are willing to make in return for the personal, private, and public benefits they receive.

Counting a museum's total engagements makes achieving diversity goals and increasing engagements more manageable in the short term. Once museums can add the engagements at a free festival to the number of visitors paying premiums for a blockbuster, they broaden participation with new audiences. The profile of a museum's total engagements may be more diverse than of its paid visitors.

USE THE PIID SEQUENCE TO MONITOR IMPACT

(Purposes → Impacts → Indicators → Data fields)

Evaluator Johnny Fraser reminded me that you don't know an outcome is happening unless you can observe it, and this led me to look for indications that desired outcomes were happening. Among the 1,025 museum survey questions in MIIP 1.0, I found a treasure trove of potential indicators.

Once a museum decides what impacts and other outcomes it is after, it can look for indicators that each outcome is happening in evaluation responses and in operating data. Evaluation methods are well established for assessing even intangible outcomes, and I encourage their use when your museum has the time and the resources. However, in one of my books,[2] I make the case for using some operating data to assess intangible outcomes when that data tracks changes in the opinions of citizen-experts, such as teachers, members, grantors, and volunteers.

Opinions can be expressed in the choices they made to exchange their time, effort, and money in museum engagements. These choices show up in the museum's operating data, among other places.

Table 12.1.   The PIID Sequence

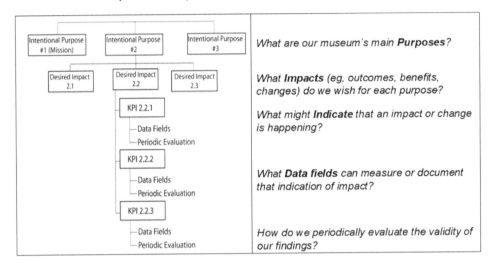

The PIID Sequence
Purposes → Impacts → Indicators → Data fields

Intentional Purpose #1 (Mission), Intentional Purpose #2, Intentional Purpose #3	*What are our museum's main Purposes?*
Desired Impact 2.1, Desired Impact 2.2, Desired Impact 2.3	*What Impacts (eg, outcomes, benefits, changes) do we wish for each purpose?*
KPI 2.2.1 — Data Fields — Periodic Evaluation	*What might Indicate that an impact or change is happening?*
KPI 2.2.2 — Data Fields — Periodic Evaluation	*What Data fields can measure or document that indication of impact?*
KPI 2.2.3 — Data Fields — Periodic Evaluation	*How do we periodically evaluate the validity of our findings?*

Changes in annual teacher renewal rates, for instance, may indicate changes in how they value the museum experience, and it may be one of the indicators a museum can monitor to assess its service to education. Periodically, the museum should also use other methods to assess its impact on teachers and revise its data choices if not supported by this second opinion. Other data fields that might assess impact can be filtered in MIIP 1.0.

Museum theory can be applied to operations through using the PIID Sequence. The sequence starts with museum leadership articulating one or more of its intentional *purposes*, then stating what changes or *impacts* the museum aspires to achieve for each purpose and what real-world observations might *indicate* that impact is happening. Then, what *data fields* might measure or document changes in that indicator. This PIID Sequence is illustrated in table 12.1.

POTENTIAL RESISTANCE

My main fear, reinforced by the AMI research project, is that the transition to more data-informed management will be slow for many in the museum profession. We are producing intangible impacts and benefits and not countable widgets. We are service organizations and not manufacturers. We are comfortable with words but not so much with numbers.

If this is the case in your museum, go slowly. Let a few exemplary successes with the use of quantitative data drive a larger shift in capacity for handling and using KPIs. Search out the quants on staff, and feed them challenges.

If, at the end of these discussions, you realize that your culture trusts the guts of your experienced staff more than the available research, it may mean you have excellent and visionary staff, but it also may mean you need to improve the quality and buy-in of your research. Because all this falls apart if the quality of the data is too poor to draw any conclusions. If a museum's managers do not trust the accuracy and consistency of the data, they will dismiss its use, claiming garbage in, garbage out (GIGO).

Resistance may also come from lack of number skills and an unfamiliarity with data management. I am always taken aback when a museum manager is not comfortable moving around Excel, for instance. MIIP 1.0 is an Excel database, and extracting value from it requires knowing how to filter and sort by criteria.

Visitor studies professionals may express concern. Data-informed management should not threaten traditional evaluation; rather, it depends on it. To test and verify assumptions about the meaning of changes in operating data, other evaluation methodologies—surveys, focus groups, interviews, and so on—are needed to understand motive: Why did more teachers come back this year? A museum might like to believe they returned because of the educational value, but maybe some other museum raised their prices.

Rock-hard resistance may come from leaders who make decisions by gut and not by data. When leadership does not believe that the choices made by audiences and supporters are relevant to the museum's decisions, then there may be little point in moving toward a data-informed organization.

INCREASED IMPACTS AND BENEFITS

For independent museums in the United States, John Falk's "free choice" means no one must go to museums much less support them. Museums must provide their audiences and supporters with value. Maybe government and university museums can count on their funding, as can a few fully endowed museums, but for most of the rest of the nonprofit museums in the United States, survival depends on providing value not only generally to the larger public good but also specifically to its audiences and supporters.

Although this existential obligation is a duty, fulfilling it, year in and year out, becomes a testament to a museum's enduring value. Museums are market-based organizations, and our customers tell us what they value by their choices to exchange their time, effort, and money for museum experiences. Listening closely to changes in yearly exchange data, especially those data fields that indicate desired outcomes, can inform management decisions in response to its community's constantly changing needs and aspirations.

An indirect yet potent corollary to using data to inform management is to use data to evidence outcomes to supporters, who may ask for such summative accounting.

Communicating consistent data to community leaders and funders will build trust and repeat business. Funders like to see results, and, increasingly, they expect to see numbers and stories as proof of impact.

Integrating your museum's research activities, identifying kindred impacts, counting more engagements annually, and using the PIID Sequence are initiatives intended to increase museum effectiveness by amplifying and organizing the responses from audiences and supporters.

STEPS TO ADAPT THE IDEAS TO YOUR MUSEUM

The first question to ask: Is your museum's leadership interested in moving toward more data-informed management? If not, ask why not. If yes, but managers are unsure of either the benefits or the methods, then move on to the next steps.

Likely, your museum has already implemented aspects of my suggestions in this chapter. Research how the museum is currently using data to assess impact, to inform management, and to communicate your results publicly. For instance, is there a museum dashboard with KPIs that managers track regularly and use? Does it track impacts as well as performance? Do you regularly report outcomes to public agencies? What problems and aspirations do managers have with current data and its usefulness?

These findings can help you adapt these four initiatives to better fit your context. You can phase them in, starting with small, proof-of-benefit steps: Add research and evaluation to a staff job description; start using *engagements* instead of *attendance*; expand advocacy and fundraising to kindred impact organizations, and try monitoring two or three impact indicators to see if they are meaningful and useful. As these tryouts pay off, expand to fuller versions of these initiatives.

Implementing any one of these initiatives should help your museum move toward a more data-informed organization. Implementing all four should set you further on the road to measuring, documenting, and communicating your impacts.

NOTES

1. The MIIP Database, an Excel workbook, is available for free online; search for "MIIP 1.0."

2. John W. Jacobsen, *Measuring Museum Impact and Performance* (Lanham, MD: Rowman & Littlefield, 2016).

13

Get Real about Financials

A part of me doesn't want to write this chapter because I am suggesting closing some financial loopholes that have helped museums in transition over the years. I found that nonprofit museums could get away with accounting practices forbidden to more normal enterprises. Museums did not need to account for depreciation as a component of their operating budgets; they seldom kept sufficient cash reserves and found some ways to use capital dollars to cover operating expenses. These exemptions allowed museums to balance their operating budgets with less operating revenue.

These loopholes often put off replacing systems and roofs and led to significant deferred maintenance costs, which later required capital campaigns. But raising those later capital dollars seemed easier than raising more operating support now. It put off meeting revenue goals in the early years, but, well, the staff was inexperienced and the expansion new, so they'll meet their goals before the campaign subsidy runs out. Besides, that's later. It meant there was little reserve to cover emergencies, but what could happen? If an emergency ever happens, it will be later.

After the lockdowns, with museums ravaged economically and the earned revenue share of their business models in tatters, and at a time when money is scarce and deferred maintenance costs increasing, I am suggesting setting money aside for a path toward fiscal responsibility. We have learned that later is now.

This chapter outlines four steps that I suggest museums should incorporate into their master plans. Collectively, the steps lead museums toward alignment with fiscal and accounting practices followed by stable organizations. Your museum may be well along in these:

- Resolve conflicts between capital and operations.
- Fund depreciation to pay for preventive maintenance and replacements.
- Phase in an adequate cash reserve and tame cash flow.
- Stop funding operations from capital and, instead, assess donations.

I also have a few pet peeves to work through in this chapter, but they are incidental, and I will weave them in.

THE PROBLEM

In my work with museums, I quickly learned two lessons probably untaught in museum studies courses: (a) Set your spending needs when starting a new job because later you'll have to bargain and wait in line to change your first year's budget; and (b) operating dollars are tight but capital dollars are looser.

I remember touring a new museum in its third year of operation, when the allure of novelty had worn off and the second-year slump in attendance and fundraising had done its damage. Large closets in the spacious yet empty education department were filled with hands-on educational resources to be used with school groups and live program demonstrations. All were unopened. There were models of the human body, terrariums to be inhabited by bees and ants, tubes of wall posters and other visual props, soil and water testing kits, and a zoo of plush animals—all in multiple sets. The program spaces were silent and the offices lonely because many of the educators had been laid off during the slump. During the confusion of opening, no one was trained to use their wealth of materials, but then they were laid off. So the closets full of capital purchases went unused.

I have many other examples where the operating dollars were not able to realize the capital phase ambitions. Yet at another museum, educators waited for a single Stuffee (an educational doll) to be approved for their next year's operating budget because it had been denied the year before.

RESOLVE CONFLICTS BETWEEN CAPITAL AND OPERATIONS

The distinction between operating dollars and capital dollars is significant, both from an accounting viewpoint and from day-to-day practice. Both should be spent with equal caution and aspiration, investing in the future of the museum and the pursuit of its purposes. However, current practice varies widely for these two kinds of money, and I believe that closing the gaps will be beneficial for both sides.

I found it is difficult to get museum managers to agree to new expenses that are not covered by their current operating budget. Managers work hard to wring the most out of their limited discretionary funds, and each expenditure is carefully guarded and considered. Capital dollars, on the other hand, once approved, are often spent rapidly, sometimes on big ticket contracts and system purchases. Buying a new admissions system can take years if purchased through the operating budget but only a few weeks in the rush of outfitting a new lobby addition.

Capital expectations do not always align with operating realities. Supporters provide capital funds in the expectation of promised outcomes, such as educational

CAPITAL AND OPERATIONS

Capital and operating dollars are distinguished by how and on what they are spent. Capital dollars are intended to cover long-term assets, such as new systems and facilities, whereas operating dollars cover day-to-day expenses such as salaries and supplies. Often, spending capital dollars requires a different approval loop from operating dollars, which are usually approved within the departmental budget and organization chart. The source and allocation of capital dollars is detailed in the *capital budget* and the operating dollars in the museum's annual *operating budget*.

A *capital project* involves the creation of a capital asset funded by a *capital campaign* that raised the capital dollars to pay for the capital project. A project typically lasts a defined *term* from the *notice to proceed* to *completion* and follows stated *project objectives* and a *scope of work*. Capital projects often overlap regular operations and can bridge fiscal years and be carried forward, unlike operating dollars that generally do not carry forward.

Transition funds are needed to cover incremental operating costs due to the capital project and need to be identified at the same time as the capital project funds. The funds cover additional costs such as precompletion staffing and occupancy costs as well as loss of revenue when capital construction compromises operating revenues. Some museums neglect to include these funds, requiring later adjustments to the operating budget.

Preopening operating and support funds: transition funds plus other noncapital expenses directly associated with the capital project, such as fundraising and marketing costs, the owner's contingencies, and escalation reserves.

Restricted and unrestricted funds: The museum is obligated to spend restricted funds only as designated by the donor, whereas the museum is free to spend unrestricted funds as it wishes.

Indirect costs: covers the museum's administrative costs (human resources, payroll, finance and accounting, management, etc.) to handle the capital project in addition to its direct capital costs. Indirect costs are often assessed to grants and donations as a negotiated or calculated percentage.

Depreciation: In standard practice, the depreciated amount in each year of a capital investment is posted as an expense in the operating budget. In pragmatic terms that means that a system costing 100 units with a 10-year life would post 10 units of expense every year for 10 years. In theory, setting aside 10 percent of the cost every year would provide a replacement sum at the end sufficient to buy a new system, adjusted for inflation by the interest earned in a growing account.

outcomes. Operating dollars, however, are earned by providing audiences with benefits that may have little to do with the educational outcomes desired by the supporters. A classic example is an exhibition funded to communicate public health messages by a pharmaceutical, while charging admission to an audience that wants a quality visitor experience and a good time with friends and family. Of course, both objectives can be accomplished, but often the content gets too dense, losing some visitors.

Museum capital projects involving significant expansions or renovations often raise money from family foundations with a promise of a legacy gift. These days, permanence is seldom promised a donor, yet the audience's expectations for change may be shorter than the donor's aspirations for longevity. Sometimes, this can translate into commitments on the capital project that compromise the operational flexibility that a museum needs to stay relevant. This is not just in gallery-naming opportunities, which can limit sponsorships, but also when the layout and content are difficult to change. After a few years, the Dinosaur Hall can become a dinosaur hall.

Matching the funders' intentions with a capital project's needs has always involved some fancy footwork to align the source of funds to the allocation of funds. Donors can stipulate how they want their funds to be spent, usually in reflection of the promises the museum has made to the donor about what the donation will achieve, such as "for the new education center," or "to endow the deputy director position." Stipulations can also exclude covering operating costs or contributing to an endowment. On the spending side, however, the allocation of funds needs to be spread among clear capital costs, such as construction and built-in equipment, while also funding intangibles, such as fundraising costs, project management, contingencies, escalation reserves, and preopening staffing costs. These are often considered unrestricted funds and are among the hardest to raise during a competitive capital campaign.

It would be useful to have a way to handle projects that are not really capital but cross over fiscal years. I suggest that accounting practices find a way to let smaller museums spend money in one fiscal year that pays back in the next year. Larger museums do this all the time, but finding the cash reserves to fund the expenses in the initial year may limit the ability of smaller museums. Deposits on future traveling exhibitions, lease down payments, and gift shop stock expansions exemplify up-front costs that are not capital investments but part of operational initiatives that bridge fiscal years. In 1988, the $4 million budget for *Ramesses the Great* had to be spent mostly the year before it opened to the public and earned back its $7 million revenue. This produced misleading financial reports those two years.

FUND DEPRECIATION TO PAY FOR PREVENTIVE MAINTENANCE AND REPLACEMENTS

I suggest that depreciation be more than just a journal entry but an actual replacement fund, added to each year as a line item in the operating budget. Not only would this help pay for replacements, but it would remind us that most of our hard capital assets are not forever but have useful lives.

Some museums do not include depreciation expenses in their operating budget and do not consider funding these costs as part of an operating need. Some consider depreciation expense as a noncash theoretical expense; instead, when faced with a system or space at the end of its useful life, they raise capital dollars for replacements or do nothing and let the aged resource limp along well beyond its time. Incurring significant levels of deferred maintenance can create a compounding effect, resulting in higher costs over time that could have been avoided by practicing regular preventive maintenance. Safety issues can also result from high levels of deferred maintenance.

Generally accepted accounting principles (GAAP) require organizations to account for depreciation on their books, and many organizations do so in a separate capitalized asset fund. The problem is organizations are not required to fund depreciation or replacement funds or reserves. Only well-managed organizations do so. This and other related issues are discussed in *Getting Beyond Breakeven*, a study by the William Penn Foundation.[1]

It is tricky but sometimes necessary to capitalize programs. The issue is that programs should change, and capital investments should be long term. Yet it is important that capital expansions open with something in them, and the money to pay for the opening set of programs in a new capital project needs to be incorporated into the fundraising goals of the project. From an accounting viewpoint, this means that the budget includes both capital expenses and preopening operating expenses.

Funding museum programs with capital dollars runs into depreciation problems due to the short life span of most programs. The high cost encourages long-term amortization of new exhibit galleries, for instance, and assuming a ten-year life for an expensive capital renovation makes the yearly expense seem more reasonable. The problem is that most exhibits lose their freshness and relevance well before ten years.

One solution, explored in chapter 8, is to separate long-term elements of exhibit galleries from changeable ones. That way the underlying experience platform layer can be amortized for five or more years while the scenarios installed on it might be expensed through the operating budget every year. This is one way of capitalizing programs. Another is to establish a fund sufficient for covering five or more years' worth of changing programs.

PHASE IN AN ADEQUATE CASH RESERVE AND TAME CASH FLOW

Prepandemic, the rule of thumb was to carry about 20 percent of your annual expense budget in cash reserves, maintaining that balance throughout normal years, and drawing down on it only for unexpected rainy days.

I wonder what directors with lockdown experience think today. During the 2020 lockdown, museum director Barry Van Deman declared "cash is king" when his museum's revenue dried up, and their cash accounts measured out their future. The more cash he could identify, the more future.

The amount of prudent cash reserve is probably a moving target, affected by the current risk assessment—in dangerous times, a higher percentage. Talk to your peers and local museums: What are their ideal and actual cash reserves as a share of annual expenses?

Augmented cash reserves also can tide a museum over periodic cash flow issues. Earned revenue in January may slump, but July's crowds make up the difference. Fine, but where do you get the money to pay February's salaries? Many businesses have lines of credit to handle such seasonal variations, but a better answer for museums is to add to the cash reserves an amount that the museum can borrow to cover seasonal shortfalls and repay later.

All this may be nice, but it assumes the museum has extra money. How are cash reserves funded? In addition to endowment funds, we used to include cash reserves as a line item in the capital and preopening budgets for new museums. That may be an option if your museum is organizing a campaign. Alternatively, you could phase in an appropriate reserve by budgeting a yearly amount to be transferred; 2 percent of the yearly expense budget would get you to 20 percent over ten years. You could also set up an account with a one-way ratchet, where any leftover and excess funds get deposited but cannot be withdrawn arbitrarily. Some museums budget operating revenue conservatively, hoping to set aside any surpluses in a rainy-day cash reserve fund.

**STOP FUNDING OPERATIONS FROM CAPITAL, AND INSTEAD,
ASSESS DONATIONS WITH INDIRECT COSTS**

Capital campaigns have impacts on operations; the question is how to cover the incremental operating costs. One answer is to disclose that some of the campaign funds will be used that way as *preopening operating funds* intended to cover incremental staff and their expenses before the capital project is finished and open to the public.

Another answer is to assess every capital donation, even restricted funds, with an *indirect cost*, typically a percentage[2] meant to cover the institution's administrative costs for handling the grant. Indirect costs are routine for many foundations, and private donors might agree to the precedent. A large museum required capital campaign donors who sponsored or funded an exhibition gallery to also fund ten years of the gallery's operating costs.

Another option, open only to larger, stabilized museums, is to buckle up and absorb all the incremental costs in the operating budget, which might be expanded during the term of the capital project.

The problem can also be an opportunity to invigorate the case for operating support. This approach to handling operating increments builds on the shift in philanthropy away from brick-and-mortar capital projects and toward funding programs with demonstrable impacts on the number of people served. Programs can have start-up costs that can be amortized over the operating run of the program, or they can be capitalized if the anticipated run is long enough. This shifts fundraising emphasis from the allure of permanence to the impact of operating results.

One of my pet peeves is calling support funding "deficit funding," with the implication that the museum's failure to raise sufficient earned revenue forces the board to cover the deficit from their own pockets.

Support funding should be mutually beneficial and not a duty that board members seek to avoid. Providing benefits to supporters does not come naturally and requires that the museum be intentional about providing value to its supporters in return for their funding. Of course, some of that value should be in social returns on investment, backed by evidence that the impacts they funded are being realized, but other valued benefits include the prestige and contacts of museum foundation membership.

POTENTIAL RESISTANCE

All these steps require setting aside hard-earned money in variously restricted accounts and just letting it sit there, when there are payroll and other pressing expenses to be paid.

Lack of money is a valid reason for not maintaining cash reserves and for finding ways to supplement operations from capital funds, but the reason, like all spending choices, reflects the museum's priorities. When the choice is setting aside cash versus letting a staffer go, museum managers often choose empathy over prudence.

And that's what I would do too. As I started this chapter, I admitted that the loopholes enabled worthy progress quickly and that I was not sure the rules should be tightened.

I now see the benefit of an economically healthy museum that funds depreciation, maintains sufficient cash reserves, establishes acceptable methods to cover impacts on operations from capital budgets, implements provisions for multiyear operating budgets, and still offers good job conditions and pay. Such a museum is also likely to be more effective at achieving its purposes than a museum playing fast with its finances.

NOTES

1. https://williampennfoundation.org/sites/default/files/reports/Getting%20Beyond%20 Breakeven_0.pdf, accessed February 26, 2022.

2. A method for calculating indirect costs for a museum contracting for a national government grant appear in section 64, table 64.9 of the *Museum Manager's Compendium*.

Plan Your Future

Let's face it, the lockdowns of March 2020 caught most museums by surprise. There were few pandemic plans and a wide variety of responses in the early weeks. Staff were furloughed, fired, or told to stay home, except for some deemed essential but put at risk. There were few plans for lockdowns to guide the hurried phone calls among directors, CFOs, and board members. Eventually, museums started talking to other museums, and some sense of shared response and operational policies grew into long-term changes. But it was not because of forethought, but hindsight. Much the same might be said for museums' response to the Great Recession and 9/11 (see chapter 15).

At the other end of the "caught blindsided" spectrum, I bet there are board members quizzing directors about why their museum did not think of the immersive Van Gogh exhibitions first. Why not immersive Francis Bacon? Hieronymus Bosch? Ad Reinhardt? Yayoi Kusama? (Wait, that's been done already.) Where are the museum field's future innovations to come from?

The truth is that many museums are not good at looking at futures different from their present. Museums have grown good at five-year master planning, but most of those assume the world will continue its current trends and that current museum program types will evolve slowly. Museums book temporary exhibitions years out and kick off multiyear capital campaigns for gallery renovations, conceived in the pre-whatever years. Often focused on the museum's programs and fighting fires daily, museum leaders seldom have time to speculate or plan for different futures, and so resign to work within present conditions. The most defeatist saying I heard from a manager was "It is what it is. Learn to love it."

Museums not only need to plan for their future disruptions but doing so will also be beneficial in the present because the process identifies actionable societal trends, inspired solutions, and fundable plans.

I consider both ends of a future risk-and-reward spectrum—crisis and innovation—after listing some of the reasons for our current status:

- Adopt crisis management response actions.
- Strengthen research and development of innovations.

THE PROBLEM

Board members, many of whom remember being called "trustees," are inherently protective of the museums they govern in public trust. In the United States, all the board members I worked with were volunteers (in Canada, some were paid). These two factors combine to make independent nonprofit museums in the United States resistant to risk and without much extra time to spend on anything but keeping the museum running. Museum finance committees typically prefer low-risk endowment funds and shy away from investing museum funds in speculative museum ventures.

The IMAX boom of the 1980s and 1990s was an exception when museums added giant screen theaters as people magnets and profit centers. But even then, boards needed to see economic feasibility studies,[1] ideally showing good rates of return on capital outlays.

Those were also the Museum Boom years (1980s–2008), when capital flowed to museum expansions. Today, there are still new museums capitalized, but for most operating museums, proposed expenses beyond the operating budget are scrutinized by need and then queued. Getting approval to invest money now in future museum innovations will be challenging.

Risk is best undertaken over strong safety nets. The museum field has some deep pockets willing to underwrite innovations. National Science Foundation, National Endowment for the Humanities (NEH), National Endowment for the Arts (NEA), and Institute of Museum and Library Services (IMLS) are among the foundations and agencies funding museum innovations, many of which resulted in workbooks, templates, and research findings available to any interested museum.

ADOPT CRISIS MANAGEMENT POLICIES

Stock market advisor Nassim Taleb coined "black swan" as an unpredictable event that might have dire consequences. He observed that afterward, folks usually say we had it coming, but Taleb says that black swans are truly unpredictable.

The pandemic lockdown, I believe, qualifies as a black swan event. We could not have predicted the March 2020 closing, though the later ones became routine. So how was a museum supposed to plan for the first one?

The first line of defense should be the cash reserves and funds described in the previous chapter; therefore, review the adequacy of your operating reserves and rainy-day funds and develop action plans as needed.

It is possible to break down responses to crises into manageable and plannable component parts so that when an unpredictable black swan happens, management can pull out whichever parts are needed. In short, you may not be able to predict the crisis, but managing it is likely to involve one or more of the following *response actions*, which you can plan ahead:

- Closing the museum
  - Closing part of the museum
- Furloughing or firing staff and contractors
- Working remotely
- Explaining museum problems publicly
- Handling a major financial shortfall
- Mourning the death of a staff member
- Detoxifying the museum
- Providing alternate access routes
- Addressing violent crowds
- Coping without the IT system
- Market and bank collapses
- Handling anything else that wakes you at 4:00 a.m.

The causes of any of these response actions might vary, but the museum should know what to do when such actions are suddenly needed. For instance, the museum's computers and IT system may be offline for many reasons: CPU failure, cabling failure, ransomware attack, operator error, and so on, but the museum's actions might be similar.

The solutions can be scaled. Closing the museum, for instance, might be for hours, days, weeks, or months, and each length might need different provisions. When I was the director on duty one Saturday, I had to evacuate some two thousand visitors within a few minutes and close the museum in response to a bomb threat, leaving only the security chief, facility manager, and me in the building, while visitors waited outside until the bomb squad arrived and swept the building. During the recent lockdowns, some thought it would be for a few weeks until it became months. Different causes and lengths, but both involve the sudden and unforeseen closing of the museum. Where do you set the thermostats? Who protects the collection? Who locks the doors and sets the alarms? Who feeds the tarantulas and toads?

Museums may not be able to anticipate black swans, but they can plan contingency actions that can be customized and collected as needed without having to wrestle with policy choices in a panic—to furlough or fire?

STRENGTHEN RESEARCH AND DEVELOPMENT

We have no lack of visionaries. Museum literature, session panels, and blog posts are full of ideas and proposed innovations. What we lack is a process to consider and concept test the most promising of these ideas. What we lack is a research and development (R&D) process for the field. Perhaps it is something like the American Alliance of Museums' (AAM's) Museum Assessment Program (MAP), where ideas are submitted to peer review and experiments resulting in a few well-considered recommendations.

In the last few decades, we've let the earned revenue market drive our innovations, resulting in new traveling exhibition galleries, visitor centers, function rental atria, and IMAX theaters. The most popular museum innovations—blockbusters, children's museums, robotic dinosaurs, *Body Worlds*, and so on—were then copied by commercial entrepreneurs. Entrepreneurs, now ahead of museums, show off their own inventive chops with high-priced immersive exhibitions of Van Gogh and others.

We might do well by shifting attention to innovations in the support revenue sector, as the entrepreneurs are less likely to follow. The Museum of Science (Boston, Massachusetts) launched its Center for Life Sciences and Public Learning (2022),[2] the first of its planned collection of learning centers, each headed by an expert and serving as a programmatic interface between Boston's vibrant economic sectors and the public. Although exhibits may be part of the program, the center can provide programs and program components in many formats and to many other platforms. There is wealth in the life sciences community as well as corporations and business groups committed to public outreach. This innovation is likely to operate largely on funding from corporate, agency, and private donors.

Not all innovations should be market driven. Not all innovations should go through a formal R&D vetting process. Some innovations are disruptive, idiosyncratic. Crises as well as brilliance drive innovations (see chapter 15). Some innovations come from individuals and some from individual museums, but for an innovation to take hold and influence the field, others need to be involved: up front to buffer the risk and, after the first sites, to embed the practice in more museums.

The museum field could use versions of business incubator organizations that exist to help start-ups through the various stages of development. The NSF Advancing Informal Stem Leaning (AISL) program has funding support available under a peer-review grant process for innovations at various stages related to informal science learning, some of which helps science, children's, and natural history museums innovate. More of this kind of support in other sectors of the museum field might catalyze significant advances in museum learning, as well as document impacts.

It would be helpful to individual museums if their board embraced the need for R&D and recognized that some degree of risk-taking is desirable, even as a prescribed policy. The corollary is that governance should expect some failures.

At a field-wide level, the backbone organizations described in chapter 7 could support innovation and buffer risk, and government agencies might provide forms of insurance to mitigate risk, modeled on their coverage of art and artifacts.[3]

POTENTIAL RESISTANCE

Limited volunteer and staff time keep board and staff focused on operations, without much time to surmise crisis scenarios. There is also the morale problem of who wants to wrestle with an emergency staff reduction plan? Emergency planning is no fun, and the last thing the planners want is to have their plans put into action. Yet, without fire escape routes pasted on every exit door, how are folks going to escape safely?

Moving a museum, much less the museum field, toward a more venturesome, experimental culture may meet resistance at each link in the chain of approval and action: Operational staff may be used to current practices; managers may be responsible for meeting existing budgets; leaders may have their marching orders; and board members may shy away from risky time demands.

Such resistance is good, I think, as risk is—and should be—unfamiliar to museum culture, grounded as we are in conservation and public service. All I am suggesting is an openness to consider risk, and a small step toward entrepreneurship.

INCREASED IMPACTS AND BENEFITS

Would crisis management have buffered the damage done by the pandemic lockdowns? Would a visionary R&D process have identified immersive media exhibitions as a potential museum innovation? I believe so, perhaps not directly or fully, but I think that preparing response actions would have made museums more resilient and investing in R&D made them more forward-looking.

STEPS TO ADAPT THE IDEAS TO YOUR MUSEUM

My suggestions for crisis management are echoed by others, and various aspects have been implemented in many museums. Your museum might start by searching for existing emergency action policies used in other museums or available on the web.

Crisis management has its own field of experts, and your museum may want to engage one to run through a checklist to assess what you have in place and what you still need to develop.

This is also a security question, and the AAM's Museum Security Committee is a good place to start (securitycommittee.org). They offer resources and PowerPoint briefings. The ASIS International site (asisonline.org), which certifies security professionals in many fields, offers deeper resources.

I have been a planner all my professional life. In a way, I worked in the future, estimating what museum x will be doing in y years when the $$z$ capital project is finished. Our master plans were written in "future positive," assuming everything will happen as planned.

We're proud of our track record and of our successfully operating museums, but I know we did not plan on crises, nor did we count on transformative innovations. Yet both happened. Good thing we had planned contingency funds.

NOTES

1. My company did many of these studies through our associate, Mark B. Peterson.

2. https://www.mos.org/press/press-releases/Dr-Insoo-Hyun-Life-Sciences-Director, accessed February 4, 2022.

3. The Arts and Artifacts Indemnity Act (P.L. 94-158) as amended (P.L. 110-161, Sec. 426) authorizes the Federal Council to make indemnity agreements with US nonprofit, tax-exempt organizations and governmental units for coverage of eligible objects owned by public and private collections in the United States, while on exhibition in the United States. https://www.arts.gov/impact/arts-and-artifacts-indemnity-program/domestic-indemnity#, accessed February 4, 2022.

Part VII
REIMAGINE
MUSEUM MODELS

Past crises over the last five decades pushed museums into new models. What models will emerge tomorrow? This book suggests the future of American community museums lies in becoming more effective programmable museums. It is really about what you do with your resources that improves the world.

15

Embrace Public Mandates

Originally I titled this chapter "Avoid Unfunded Mandates." I was grumpy about all the good-hearted people who lectured us on what museums ought to be doing without thinking about who would pay for their oughts or how those oughts might drive away existing audiences and supporters. They spoke as if museums had free will and could decide on their own how to spend their funding and change their tune.

Over the years, I have heard that museums *ought to* (sometimes, *must*) address energy crises, universal access, security, climate change (née, global warming), green buildings and portfolios, gender equity, repatriation, income inequality, social justice, patriarchy, and racism. Few of these worthy public communications campaigns aligned with what a museum's existing audiences and supporters were paying for.

"The new museum ought to feature Bishop Fulton J. Sheen's nationally broadcast church sermons. You know he was a local man, and his sermons inspired millions of radio listeners back in the day," suggested a participant in a community workshop. Aside from all the reasons we did not include this idea in that museum's plans, the word *ought* stuck with me. The participant thought the future museum had a responsibility to tell certain stories, regardless of suitability to the medium, appeal to audiences, sensitivity to others, or relevance to the times.

I found that with every national crisis comes demands for museums to respond to a new round of oughts. Museums generally do respond but often without new funding.

As the weather extremes expand and the nation's angers boil, the pressures and changes roiling the museum field today may be stronger than the previous crises in our field. Yet we can learn from the previous disruptions and crises: How did they affect museums? Good or bad changes? Lasting or transient?

I thought a museum's primary responsibility was to deliver quality services to those who were paying for them. It was irresponsible if not unethical to use their money for other purposes. If families were paying a museum for quality time with friends and family, the museum should not use that money instead to respond to unfunded mandates.

I had the sense that I had lived through these kinds of pressures on the museum field before, so I set out to do my own research, not so much on the internet but in my own memory banks, flawed and biased though they may be.

I was surprised by what I found. I was wrong. Museums have a higher priority, and we're better for it. Serving our audiences and supporters, although important to our survival, is secondary to serving our society in its entirety.

I've singled out seven external disruptions and crises that I remember affecting museums. Each disruption caused museums to stop, rethink museum practices, and rebuild better, more resilient, and responsive museums.

Step back with me as I walk from museum evolution to museum evolution. The oldest among you will remember my start in the 1970s, and the younger will recognize the progression later in the museum field's evolution.

As I remember them, each of these disruptions and crises were tough on museums, but museums emerged better:

- New Technologies in a Time of Turmoil (1967–1980)
- Reagan's Go-Go Years (1981–1987)
- Nervous 1990s (1987–2001)
- Under Attack (2001–2005)
- The Great Recession (2008–2009)
- Trouble Brewing (2010–2019)
- The COVID-19 Pandemic

This is a personal collection. No other seasoned museum professional will select the same turning points or see history the same way. Each crisis, however, caused us to rethink museum practices, and, as a cockeyed optimist, I believe each evolution enriched museums and made them more valuable to the public. You may well have a different opinion.

In this chapter, my definition of *museums* is even narrower than other chapters. Here I am recalling the history of museums that I knew about, a tiny sample of America's museums. The museums I was aware of tended to be the larger, city-based museums in the main disciplines: art, science, natural history, regional history, zoos, aquariums, and children's museums.

NEW TECHNOLOGIES IN A TIME OF TURMOIL (1967–1980)

The first disruptions for museums that I remember occurred in the 1970s: Political upheaval, Watergate and the Vietnam War, school busing and rioting, a recession, and rampant inflation resulted in economic and cultural pressures on independent museums in the United States. Two of the decade's disruptions—the energy crises and the challenges from a new generation of commercial cultural attractions—have stayed with me for their influence on museum practice.

The gas crisis of 1973 curtailed long car trips, altering tourism and reducing school trips, and the oil crisis of 1979 raised deeper questions about our growing energy dependence. Would our love of technology save us or kill us?

Civic leaders thought natural history and science museums ought to increase public awareness of the sources and costs of energy, and many did. The Museum of Science (Boston, Massachusetts), for instance, opened the *Energy: Crisis and Challenge* exhibit in 1978. Larry Bell, who worked on the exhibit team at the time, describes it as the largest and most comprehensive exhibit the museum had mounted. It included a bowling ball roller coaster, a pyramid of oil barrels, a cutaway home wall showing insulation, and interactive displays on a variety of energy topics and sources. A multiscreen, computer-controlled, multimedia presentation about possible energy futures screened in the adjacent Wright Theater, but visitors avoided the show, and it was dropped well before the rest of the exhibit was replaced in 1994. Oughts can sometimes fade, I learned, and ought not to be the content of permanent exhibits.

The new wave of commercial attractions, however, stimulated a long-term museum evolution.

In 1972 the Salem Witch Museum (Salem, Massachusetts) opened with an indoor sound and light show using scenery and mannequins to narrate the history of the 1492 witch trials. In 1973, the Boston Tea Party Ships and Museum opened, and, among the standing text panels, a Kodak Carousel slide projector clicked through a tray of images while a MacKensie repeater played Mason Williams's "Classical Gas" over and over. Both are still profitable, privately owned commercial ventures.

By the country's bicentennial, *Where's Boston?* (Prudential Plaza, Boston, 1975) drew audiences with banks of forty carousels clicking through 3,100 slides to a quadraphonic soundtrack, and *The Whites of their Eyes* (Raytheon Pavilion, Boston, 1974) immersed audiences in seven-track dimensional sound, animated slide projections plus lighting, scenery, and costumed figures to tell the history of the Battle of Bunker Hill.

Slide projectors appeared in planetariums, and museums developed audiovisual departments, using video and projections to enhance exhibits. Museums evolved to include media technologies among our other tools. Along for the ride, soon came storytelling and its mate, emotion.

During this time, another disruptive technology influenced museums. New approaches to hands-on interactivity spread in museums from its 1969 installations at the Exploratorium (San Francisco, California) and the Ontario Science Centre

(Toronto, Ontario). In the 1970s, these new approaches to hands-on exhibits first spread to other science museums and children's museums, and eventually interactive spaces appeared in art and history museums.

In the 1970s, the popularity of new media technologies and approaches to exhibits pushed museums to evolve toward places where visitors could experience stories and learn interactively. The relevance of energy content ebbed, but the tools of media technologies and hands-on activities landed in museums.

REAGAN'S GO-GO YEARS (1981–1987)

The next disruption that I think affected museums' evolution was the entrepreneurial bravado and deregulation during the main Reagan years, from his inauguration in 1981 to Black Monday in 1987. This disruption was not as sudden as many of the others on my list, but it forever changed the business models of many US independent nonprofit museums to pursue visitor-based revenues. With an uneasy relationship to the growth of earned revenue, education grew as a museum purpose and resulted in staff departments and catalogs of museum classes.

Acknowledging this evolution in museum purposes long in the making, in 1984 the American Association of Museums published *Museums for a New Century*, which stated that education was the prime purpose of museums. Conserving collections—the foundation of many established museums—was still important but should serve education.

Education departments expanded in the 1980s, sometimes in tension with curatorial departments, to interpret a museum's collections and permanent exhibits to visitors and program participants. Museum educators liaised directly with schoolteachers, tailoring programming to their curricula.

The 1980s were the Reagan years, also known as the go-go years, when the economy was hot and entrepreneurship prized. Deregulated businesses expanded and joined a merger and acquisitions heyday. Museums jumped on the bandwagon with the growth of earned revenue and its enablers, branding and marketing. Earned revenue came from paying visitors to ever-fancier visitor experiences and blockbuster exhibitions, lured by the memories of the national tour of the *Treasures of Tutankhamun* (1976 to 1979).

Anticipating even larger crowds, museums built new lobbies, changing exhibition galleries, gift shops, immersive theaters, restaurants, and fancy atria to host events and galas, kicking off a boom in new museums and expansions that was to last until the Great Recession (2008).

The growth of education and of earned revenue intersected in paid programs, often independent from the museum's galleries, but taking place in newly capitalized education and learning centers, equipped with program spaces, studios, labs, and workshops separate from the galleries. Education departments ran camp-ins, family workshops, youth classes, and outreach programs, sometimes profitably. Programs began to give museums options outside the galleries. Museums were becoming more than just their public galleries.

Museums were hot. In 1988, the Museum of Science (Boston, Massachusetts) counted 2.2 million on-site visits to the museum, full of interactive exhibits and media. More than a million dollars of marketing investment drew them to the expanded Exhibit Halls, Mugar Omni Theater, Charles Hayden Planetarium, and Nichols Gallery, which hosted the blockbuster *Ramesses the Great* that summer. Attendance never again reached that peak.

THE NERVOUS 1990s (1987–2001)

On Black Monday, October 19, 1987, the stock market crashed, and leveraged investors raced to cover margin calls. The Savings and Loan (S&L) crisis unfolded late in the 1980s and early in the 1990s, saddling the country with bad debts based on wishful thinking. The market recovered eventually, but the go-go years were gone, and the S&L laxity meant it was time to question assumptions.

The boom in new museums continued, but attendance plateaued as the novelty of interactivity and media immersion receded. In estimating attendance potentials, my company saw the trends and adjusted the numbers downward, as we did in the 1990s for the New England Aquarium's Simons IMAX Theatre (Boston, Massachusetts), which opened in 2001 as the third IMAX in the same market, soon followed by more IMAXs. Everyone, it seemed, wanted to ride the attendance wave just as the novelty ebbed and the number of competitors flowed.

New museums were built to symbolize their region and enliven downtown developments. Museum capital projects promised cachet and foot traffic to real estate developers, culture to community leaders, economic development to governments, and higher quality of life to residents. Conceived in the 1990s, but a decade in development, the new Tech Museum of Innovation along with the Children's Museum of San Jose symbolized Silicon Valley's success and identity.

Not everyone was happy with the museum craze for earned revenue. It skewed attendance toward the rich, it tarnished a museum's august authority, and it portrayed museums as greedy mercenaries. Profiting off education seemed somehow wrong to many committed educators. Were museums selling out? Were some audience segments excluded?

Late in 1990, Congress passed the Native American Graves Protection and Repatriation Act (NAGPRA), which recognized that museums held some objects illegally taken from American Indians that should be returned. The repatriation movement expanded to include colonial plunders and archaeological appropriations. This disruption cast museums as receivers of stolen goods, with the victims often the globe's poorer, weaker peoples.

The American Associations of Museums' *Excellence and Equity* publication in 1992 expressed the growing concern that museums needed to be both the keepers of excellence and the champions of equity. "Excellence" was a bow to the connoisseurs of the past and "equity" to the demographics of the future. A growing diverse and multicultural public challenged the dominance of rich white men in the governance and curatorship of museums.

In response, museums developed outreach programs and school tours to engage underserved audiences. Boards sought women and Blacks. Museums paid attention to gender and racial equity in hiring interviews, board makeup, and audience development. Temporary exhibits and feature films allowed museums to include diverse faces and cultural content, but they were still produced mostly by white men.

Museums were no longer on a pedestal, immune to criticism. Museums, I found, went into a more defensive mode. Recognizing a past of elitism, museums had shifted toward popular, visitor-drawing experiences, but those were for well-educated, wealthier audiences. Some popular visitor experiences such as live orca and dolphin shows, demeaning dioramas, collections with troubled provenance, and the later plastinated body exhibitions drew museums into ethical battles.

The get-rich spirit and frothy valuations of technology firms during the 1990s ended in March 2000, when the dot-com bubble burst. Because of the decade's pressures, however, museums evolved to care about broadening participation when overall attendance growth was softening and when ethical considerations suggested changes in museum practices.

UNDER ATTACK (2001–2005)

The early years of this century share two attacks on the United States: 9/11 by terrorists, and Katrina by Mother Nature. Both affected museums.

The suicidal terrorist attacks on the World Trade Centers in New York City on September 11, 2001, shut down museums across the nation. Liberty Science Center (Jersey City, New Jersey), right across the Hudson River from the smoldering remains, opened its grounds and lobby for grieving. Mourners gathered to share their shock and emotions, demonstrating that museums could do much more for their community than just informal education.

It would be years before museum attendance, tourism, and travel volumes returned, but in that time, museums made significant enhancements to their security. With Transportation Security Administration (TSA) airport screenings suddenly the law, some museums added security gates, and most museums tightened their defenses.

The idea that terrorists could be among us, bombing our most sacred sites, kept many people away from the country's icons, including museums. Not only visitors but board members and staff also urged museums to be more cautious, more protective, and even more secure conservators of the country's treasures.

It took a few years for the new normal to become normal, and then in 2005 Hurricane Katrina flooded New Orleans and museums were flooded with a new wave of oughts.

The Aquarium of the Americas (New Orleans, Louisiana) and other nearby museums closed, and New Orleans's tourist market disappeared overnight. The devastation and displacement caused by extreme weather brought the country's attention yet again to the issues of climate change. Although it was not the first warning, Katrina certainly was dramatic, photogenic, and filled with emotional stories.

Museums in other cities offered help, and many museums reviewed their own flooding and weather-related vulnerabilities.

Museums were urged to address the existential question of our time, climate change and the destruction of our environment, and some responded with exhibits and lectures. Zoos and aquariums promoted conservation of the environment and allied with other green environmental action groups to increase awareness of the fragility of our natural environment. PIC-Green, the American Association of Museums' professional community for greener museums, was formed in 2007 with more than a hundred museum professionals signing up. Museum leaders such as Emlyn Koster and Richard Janes thought museums ought to inform the public of the danger ahead and of the kinds of steps that might avert it.

MacGillivray Freeman Films produced IMAX film *Hurricane on the Bayou* with spectacular cinematography of the flooding, damages, and rescues. The film illustrated graphically how insensitive development along the Mississippi River led to the current catastrophe. *Hurricane on the Bayou*, however, did not draw crowds in many museums. Oughts are not always popular.

This instinct to protect museums from attack by terrorists highlighted the symbolic role that museums play in their communities. The urge to use museums to engage the public in environmental action attests to a faith in museum influence. These silver linings reminded leaders that a city's museums were recognized internationally as centers of regional identity and accomplishment and trusted platforms for key messages, as well as major investments in their community's social capital. Museum buildings, often in prominent locations and in iconic architecture, were treasures to be protected for what they mean to the United States, as well as for the collections within, the values they exemplify, and the stories they tell.

THE GREAT RECESSION (2008–2009)

Museums suffered economically during the Great Recession (2008–2009), one of the worst global downturns and economic bad news since the Depression. The *Informal Learning Review* dedicated several issues to stories and tallies of job losses and museum closures. Attendance and rentals were down and, therefore, earned revenue, but endowment income was down even more, as the market had crashed.

The 2009 American Association of Museums conference in Philadelphia was full of stories of senior curators and other longtime employees seeking new work. It was more than just a cleaving of the museum workforce, however. The Museum Boom was over. And many more jobs were lost in the museum service sector as architectural firms, exhibit design companies, and fabricators were left with high overheads built up over decades of high-profile, big-budget museum capital projects. Some were able to pivot to new museum projects in China and the Middle East.

Projects under construction at the time of the crash were able to open, such as the Peoria Riverfront Museum (Peoria, Illinois) in 2010, but new projects had little hope of finding the tens if not hundreds of millions needed to build significant new museums. The proposed new Boston Museum was first forced by several factors to scale back from a spectacular Moshe Safdie design to a compromise design and then to give up on an even much smaller project.

As a result, the museum field shifted from large brick-and-mortar projects to program initiatives, tracking a change in philanthropy toward outcome-based social programs.

This was an evolution in fundraising from the days of the Museum Boom when many downtown museums expanded their exhibit halls and added new components, funded by capital campaigns that included both public funding and private philanthropy. Public funding often came from government pork-barrel legislation. Private philanthropy was motivated by legacy projects that would carry family names into the future and by honoring significant community leaders. Those sources and motivations declined with the Great Recession, and so museums had to evolve new ways to attract public and private supporters and funding.

Programs were one answer: They were more operational than capital projects, so they helped the museum's operating budget rather than fought it, and they had the potential to result in quantifiable social outcomes.

After the Great Recession, few of our museum clients wanted to expand. There were still capital projects to increase the efficiency and use of existing spaces, but not the grand ambition that had fueled the Museum Boom. If anything, our clients aspired to rethink the resources they had. Reinvention master plans that emphasized operational programs and new ways of thinking about museum engagements allowed museums to move in exciting directions without requiring huge capital investments.

Programmatic ideas with social outcomes sparked the imagination instead of starchitect new wings.

Nina Simon's book *The Participatory Museum* (2009) captured a growing interest in the people museums were serving as well as those people who museums were not reaching. The idea of a participatory museum recognized that the museum experience could be a two-way interaction between the audience and the museum. Simon's influential book and subsequent museum blogs listed many participatory tactics, such as comment boards in exhibitions, citizen advisory panels, oral history stations, voting on collection acquisitions, and numerous other techniques for involving the public in the museum's content.

Perhaps spoiled by their recent capital splurges, museums had to quickly rethink their activities, curtail spending, and look inward to the resources they still had during the Recession. Museums evolved to emphasize programs and to pay even more attention to engaging their potential audiences.

TROUBLE BREWING (2010–2019)

Social unrest influenced museums in the early 2010s. The Occupy Wall Street (2011) and the Black Lives Matter (2013 and later) movements called attention to the wealth gap between many museum board members and the general public, as well as the whiteness of most museum governance and staff.

In those years, museums also had to adapt to social media, realizing the necessity of engaging a younger generation in their own language. Museums found that their audiences had voices and opinions that could sway potential visitors.

All these factors increased the attention on visitors and the community's interests. For museums to play a role in addressing the social challenges of inequity, first they needed to clean house, and, in a 2014 article in *Curator*, I suggested museums might preach less and, with more humility, focus on providing needed services to their communities.

Trump's election in 2016 shocked me and many of my museum colleagues. His heartless distain for others, his boorish behavior, and his denial of truth and science flew in the face of museum values. This man did not sound like a friend of museums.

Nonprofit and government museums, by principle and law, should be neutral to politics, but the resistance movement and the pink pussy hat parades enjoined museums to become activists. Some museums worked a borderline defensibly "above" political divisions by championing democracy and voting registration drives. Climate change programs and green practices in museums, once educational, became political, however.

In October 2017, actress Ashley Judd started a wave of sexual harassment claims with her charges against Harvey Weinstein. The #MeToo movement drew national attention to workplace inequities. Already under pressure to diversify, museums faced harsher public scrutiny about gender and racial equity in their board, staff, and audiences.

Shortly after Trump's election, Elizabeth Merritt in her *Center for the Future of Museums* blog, reported on a survey finding that museum professionals were overwhelmingly Democrats.[1] Only a tenth of museum directors, only a twentieth of curators, and none of the art conservators in the survey were Republicans. Merritt had the bravery to ask, if we care so much about being inclusive and representing the community, where are the Trump voters in our ranks? And what about our audiences? Wilkening Consulting found that conservatives and liberals were about equally likely to have visited a museum recently.[2] Although I trust this data, I haven't seen many MAGA hats in museums or museums resisting Dr. Fauci's recommendations.

The social disruptions of this era—Occupy Wall Street, Black Lives Matter, and the Trump election—raised difficult questions for museums and signaled trouble ahead. Museums had some explaining to do, and some adjustments.

One evolution, slow in progress and uneven among museums, was another shift in museum purpose. Museums were still educational, but the content was shifting from the message stated in the museum's mission to the relevance and wants of its community—from a missionary museum to a community service museum.

During the prepandemic Trump years, museums also evolved into quiet activists, not so much advocating for political candidates as much as advocating for accuracy, science, rule of law, representative democracy, and other core American principles we thought were above politics but apparently aren't.

THE COVID-19 PANDEMIC (2020–2022)

In its impact on museums, none of these crises and social changes equaled the tsunami of the COVID-19 pandemic lockdowns of 2020–2022. Long-simmering pressures erupted when museums suddenly shut down, furloughing, firing, or sending home the diverse staff so recently hired. George Floyd's murder turned pressure into anger, with museums accused of racism and paternalism. Museum professionals, many out of work, decried workplace conditions and pay scales. The Art Institute of Chicago dissolved its volunteer docent program in 2021 because amateurs who did not need money took work from professionals who did, and, as a group, the docents did not reflect community diversity.

Remaining staff struggled to define what it would take to reopen. Hand sanitizers and one-way paths. Social distancing and masks. Is this the end of hands-on exhibits? Will anyone ever want to crowd into a blockbuster again? Do we really need to install ultraviolet lighting inside the museum's air ducts? How much money do we have left? Who is going to pay for these health mandates?

The search for answers to these unprecedented questions brought museums together to compare possible public safety solutions and reopening strategies. Federal support was critical but also new. Suddenly, it was as easy for a museum manager to Zoom with managers at other museums as it was to meet with staff. Such intermural sharing may pave the way for deeper relationships among museums (see chapter 7).

These disruptions came with a nation divided by politics and misinformation spread over fragmented social media. Museums, once one of the country's most trusted sources of information, witnessed these lies flying around, damaging health and our democracy. Some museums hosted vaccination sites and COVID testing kiosks, and others issued statements supporting science and election results but with little impact on the national schism.

Undermining traditional museum authority was the charge of paternalistic racism, leveled at museum boards, donors, and docents with some justice despite good intentions and modest improvements in diversity over the past decades. Even well-meaning museums had courted rich white men with cloudy financial provenance. Museums dependent on serving both their audiences and supporters found existential tension between their two constituents. Could we continue to serve them both? As I write this book, the museum field remains embroiled in the soul searching around racism and the need for diversity, equity, accessibility, and inclusion (DEAI) in all aspects of museum life.

Frontline museum staff and specialists protested their workplace conditions and low pay. In the face of upper managers pulling in six-figure salaries, some museum professionals unionized to negotiate more job security and living wages. One blog suggested that floor staff were better representatives of the community and that museum management should follow their ideas and values. Another noted that selling off a Michelangelo sculpture could have saved more than a hundred jobs at the Royal Academy of Arts. It is hard to predict the future specifics, but the museum workforce is evolving, and the former top-down hierarchy may be challenged.

Public interest groups have heightened sensitivity toward all cultures. Museums used to depict peoples from different times and geographies in anthropological exhibits. Now we see the underlying assumption that these peoples were "others" than our white, Western "more civilized" culture. Even the steps museums took to engage specific populations, such as a Cinco de Mayo festival to attract Mexican Americans, implied an "othering" of Mexican Americans, suggesting that the museum's normal activities were for its white regulars.

This pressure to erase stereotypes and categorization coexists with a pressure for museums to cover unrecognized stories and interpret other identities. Many historic houses now interpret the enslaved people connected in the past, while those who enslaved them are taken off their pedestals. Some museums recognize the indigenous peoples who own their land. Sexual and gender identities become topics for museum programs, allowing museums to be inclusive.

These factors have heightened a museum's role as a symbolic platform for identity affirmation and celebration.

During all these pandemic challenges and questions, one question opened up new possibilities for museum programming: How do museums do their work when their buildings are closed?

The speedy growth of digital and other off-site programming and partnerships is a clear answer pursued by many museums, and in my opinion, the direction museums have been following for years toward a program-based museum (see chapters 6 and 16). Once gallery attendance plateaued in the 1990s and once the Great Recession slowed adding more gallery space, growth in program participation was the next frontier. Prior to the pandemic, we found that the annual count of participants in scheduled programs typically was a tenth of the gallery visits. I suggest that ratio will increase dramatically both as gallery attendance declines from prepandemic levels and as scheduled programs fill up.

The business model for digital and off-site programming has yet to evolve into a sustainable activity generating enough revenue to cover its costs, much less support the cost of running the museum's building. Museums, I am confident, will find a way. The mandate to broaden participation geographically and demographically is, like the others, unfunded. Even so, we must do it.

I hope that the January 6, 2021, insurrection and storming of the Capitol and its aftermath convinced any museums left on the fence to become active in defense of democracy and truth. Yet again, another unfunded mandate coming atop a crisis. Yet again, museums must respond and evolve.

Just as the disruptions during the pandemic were severe economically, politically, culturally, and racially, so too are the evolutionary impacts on museums. White men are now at a disadvantage applying for museum management jobs, but as a colleague said, "We've had our good run." Museums evolved to be even more activist in areas of public health and social justice. By necessity, museums evolved to accommodate curtailed and changed business models as on-site attendance revenue disappeared and virtual programming soared but without clear funding. Pressures on workplace equity and pay scales increased costs just when revenue was cratering. Federal pandemic subsidies helped temporarily, but the number of full-time professionals working in museums may never return to prepandemic levels unless the evolution toward more programs can fill the gap.

In my opinion, the longest-lasting evolution in museum practice from the pandemic disruptions was to expand a museum's services well beyond communicating its disciplinary message and hosting visitors in its galleries. Museums are evolving to be multipurpose organizations serving multiple audiences in multiple ways through professional staff and governance that represent the audiences they wish to serve.

SUMMATION

By late in the 1980s, many museum galleries had evolved from collection displays to educational exhibits to media-enriched, interactive visitor experiences. Attendance and earned revenue blossomed . . . for a few years, at least. Education began its steady climb toward today's program-rich museums. The Museum Boom poured capital and innovations into the museum field, riding a wave of popularity and urban development.

Yet, perhaps because of this visibility, the 1990s started challenging museums on ethical grounds dealing with returning stolen goods and addressing gender and racial equity. The events of 9/11 and Katrina wrenched the United States awake to our fragility, and museums evolved to increase security while discovering new social services as respected symbols and common ground for community gathering.

The Great Recession hit many museum professionals and sent economic shock waves through the museum field. Capital projects dried up, and even operating budgets were stressed. In this economy, museums evolved further toward private and government-funded programs. The social unrest of the 2010s moved museums toward activism and community service, while continuing to press museums toward greater inclusion.

All these historic disruptions enabled and may have caused museum evolutions. All caused tension, if not personal losses, but none compared to the impacts the COVID-19 pandemic had on museums and museum professionals. At great pain, museums have evolved during the pandemic to share more with other museums, launch new kinds of digital and other programming, work toward DEAI in practice, revise racist and paternalistic practices, expand a museum's symbolic role in identity inclusion and environmental conservation, and become multipurpose museums serving multiple audiences and supporters in multiple ways as well as serving society as a whole.

This "serving society as a whole" is my learning outcome from this research into museum history via my memory banks and experience. The often-wrenching evolutions museums have gone through were responding to social changes in both the economy and the culture. The Salem Witch Museum and the Boston Tea Party Ships and Museum are commercial attractions, and they do not have to serve society as a whole.

Museums do. And we're better for it.

A SUGGESTION

With all that background, I finally come to my suggestion in this chapter, but it is brief: Embrace public mandates when they come from multiple sources and are clear and passionate. Chances are good they are urging your museum to evolve, and if the past is an indication, your museum will be better for the evolution.

I suggested in the previous chapter having a process and a contingency fund for dealing with crises. What I now add is to be prepared to evolve in response to significant disruptions. There is bound to be resistance and damage, but in the end, museums ought to embrace public mandates.

NOTES

1. https://www.aam-us.org/2016/11/14/healing-the-partisan-divide/, accessed February 20, 2022.

2. http://www.wilkeningconsulting.com/uploads/8/6/3/2/86329422/wlk_museum_visitor _demographic_data_story_tagged.pdf, accessed February 20, 2022.

Integrate the Suggestions

It is remarkable that so many museums survived the pandemic lockdowns. The American Alliance of Museums (AAM), extrapolating the results of a survey of its members in October 2020, described the crisis: Half the member museums had furloughed or laid off staff, and 30 percent of staff were out of work. On average, museums anticipated losing 35 percent of their operating income in 2020 and an additional 28 percent the next year. With budgets and attendance slashed, almost a third of the member museums feared closing.[1]

The crisis wrought wrenching change to museums and their human and fiscal resources, while their expensive physical resources—buildings, collections, exhibits—shifted from value-generating assets to draining liabilities.

Yet most museums survived.

The tens of thousands of campaigns, across the field and globe, to save each museum strengthened my faith in the museum field. I congratulate the museums on making it through! I am impressed by the creativity and drive of the current generation of museum professionals. You faced the challenges with innovations, particularly with new kinds of programs and new ways of serving your communities, and you acted with a speed and flexibility uncommon in my experience with prepandemic museum culture. I credit this survival to a passion for social justice coupled with a newfound willingness to make big changes. The forecast, in my opinion: better and more democratic museums.

It was a scramble and a huge amount of work. I'm sure there were blind alleys and mistakes. Emotions and abuses. Worries and angers. I suspect no one wants to relive the pandemic lockdowns of 2020–2021.

Ahead, there are many reasons for hope. Not only did museums evolve to survive, but communities, agencies, and governments also fought for our museums.

I sense in recent museum literature that more change is needed before the museum field truly adapts the innovations and lessons learned during the pandemic into rethought museum practices. My suggestions in this book offer new ways of operating museums. Some suggestions may seem like a lot of work and too great a change, yet pandemic history shows that big changes are possible and approachable in steps.

If you and some others find a suggestion appealing, then you might try some initial steps, and if they are promising, go further. This process of incremental change can be creative and collaborative. Being on such journeys with your peers is a worthy learning and relationship-building experience on its own.

RELATIONSHIPS AMONG THE SUGGESTIONS

The suggestions in this book can be considered independently. Every museum is different with different needs, current conditions, and staff culture. Only a few of my suggestions may be immediately relevant to an individual museum. Some may already operate as I suggest; for others, the idea is too far away from their current practice. This is fine, and I have organized and indexed the main suggestions and their sections to allow easy access to individual ideas. Please share these sections with your colleagues to start conversations about whether the suggestion makes sense in your museum.

On the other hand, integrating all the suggestions describes a new museum model that I call *The Effective Museum*, planned from the ground up to maximize the use of its public resources to deliver effective benefits to its audiences, supporters, and communities. That base model can be taken a step further to address how those benefits are delivered to the public: *The Programmable Museum*.

THE EFFECTIVE MUSEUM

First, imagine a fully realized *Effective Museum*, as proposed in this book's first fifteen chapters. Each paragraph summarizes a chapter's main idea and its desired impact:

1. Like many other US museums, the Effective Museum is a unique organization with a unique business model that serves its communities in multiple ways, as guided by its principles. The Effective Museum has established a few prioritized intentional purposes, which clarifies the main services, honors them with attention, and tracks their data to increase the quality and impact of each service. To unify its efforts, the museum pays constant attention to its guiding principles to stay true to its character and brand identity.
2. The Effective Museum is governed by a board of directors that is empowered to establish policy for the museum. To reduce conflicts of interest and increase audience representation, the board has delegated fundraising to a charitable foundation, whose members lead and participate in annual and capital fundraising campaigns. This division provides the museum's supporters with the benefits they seek and spreads the volunteers' workload.

3. In recognition of the competitive marketplace for both earned and support revenues, the museum has consolidated its marketing and development forces into an external relations department charged with developing relationships, motivating engagements, and generating all operating revenues.

4. The museum holds regular conversations among its staff and stakeholders to make sure everyone is focused on providing the museum's main audiences and supporters the benefits they seek. Museum staff make sure the museum's key customers are well taken care of within the museum's guiding principles, before embarking on other mandates and worthy causes.

5. The museum's board of directors and its professional staff are made up of representatives of the audiences the museum wants to serve to deliver effective programs that reflect the interests, needs, and aspirations of the museum's desired audiences.

6. The museum focuses on producing programs for the museum's public physical and virtual spaces. It organizes its staff into six departments: Administration, Planning, Production, External Relations, Operation, and Research and Evaluation—leading to greater efficiency, innovation, flexibility, increased earned and support revenues, expanded audiences and supporters, and continuous community relevance. The museum thinks systematically about programs along with their intended audiences and business models.

7. The museum shares programs and operating data with its peer museums for mutual benefit, reducing costs while increasing quality and freshness. The museum benefits from research findings using consistent data definitions and interpretation provided by backbone organizations that support the museum field as a whole.

8. The museum has invested in its current spaces to make them more productive, creating independent access zones for off-hour uses, allowing some spaces to operate in multiple modes, installing infrastructure to facilitate content change, and outfitting a few highly flexible spaces capable of dramatic conversions. These investments allow the museum to earn more revenue, serve different audiences at different times, and change content more frequently for less effort and money.

9. The museum has additional income independent of its main activities because it followed a process to discover and leverage its previously undeveloped capital resources, which now generate regular net capital asset revenue in addition to regular operating revenue.

10. To stay fresh and to regularly renew its programs, the museum staff is trained and equipped to engage creative contractors, as do many other creative sectors, more personally and less competitively. The ability to expand its core staff with regular contractors already familiar with the museum's guiding principles increases their program's effectiveness and decreases its design and production issues.

11. The museum is active when its audiences are active, using special access zones to use program spaces when the rest of the museum is closed. The museum develops its yearly program schedule and selection of offerings in response to when its audiences are available and interested in programs. In addition to in-house program production, the museum routinely and economically installs new programs produced by other museums and museum suppliers. The museum is an active member of multiple networks sharing different kinds of programs for different kinds of audiences, all supported by business models administered centrally.

12. The museum uses data comparisons and socioeconomic trends to document likely changes in impact, provide new insights, identify best practices, set staff objectives, and make more effective decisions. The museum's annual tally of its engagements from all galleries and programs provides evidence of its diverse menu of programs and engaged audiences due to offering high-quality programs that change frequently.

13. The museum has adopted financial management practices used by many other businesses that are often forgiven for nonprofit museums. The museum maintains cash reserves, funds its depreciation to pay for preventive maintenance, and has fiscal policies to handle the distinctions between capital and operating dollars. As a result, the museum is financially stable and resilient.

14. The museum has prepared crisis management options to help the managers on duty make quick emergency decisions when an unpredictable crisis forces action. On the positive side, the museum pursues innovations in museum practice by actively investing in research and development.

15. The Effective Museum has survived crisis after crisis because each time it embraced the change demanded by the crisis and evolved in response. Rather than resist each crisis, the Effective Museum found ways to adapt by providing new kinds of public services within its guiding principles.

Collectively, the previous fifteen chapters describe an idealized, content-neutral Effective Museum. How many of the descriptions already apply in some degree to your museum?

THE PROGRAMMABLE MUSEUM

Next, put this abstract ideal in operation by imagining *The Programmable Museum*.

Imagine a museum that achieves its mission and purposes by using its resources to produce and present public programs. All its activities are programs. Engagements with this museum's programs produce valued outcomes (i.e., impacts and benefits) both for the audiences and the supporters, in return for their earned and support revenues.

It is not about your resources but about what you do with those resources that changes lives. It is not about your museum's building or its collections or even its staff; it is about what the museum does with those resources, or, in my language, how the museum programs its resources. The Programmable Museum changes lives through its programs.

Most museums already program some of their spaces: Temporary exhibit galleries are programmed years in advance with a succession of traveling and temporary exhibitions, and laboratories and classroom spaces are programmed daily for different youth and adult programs, resulting in a yearly occupancy schedule.

DEFINITIONS 16.1

THE PROGRAMMABLE MUSEUM

Program (verb): to decide what to do with a space: How will you program this gallery? the museum's website?

Program (noun): (1) the intended use of a space: "What is the architectural program for the building?" "The 150 NSF Security Office should overlook the 450 NSF Loading Dock." (2) the planned museum activity in that space: "The long-term program for the East Gallery is *Birds of the Northeast*." "Tonight's program in the Grand Atrium is the Raytheon Holiday Party." I use *program* broadly: Staff running a school tour is a program, as is the run of a film and a series of ceramic studios. A research grant to study some aspect of the collection is a program, and a function rental is a program.

Workshops, studios, classes, laboratories, encounters, camps, events, functions, school tours, outreach, and *virtual engagements* are *scheduled programs* distinguished from visitor experience programs by being scheduled in time and place and typically facilitated by a museum-connected trained guide.

A programmable museum is a museum set up to plan, produce, and operate programs in its public spaces throughout the year. The model assumes that its public spaces (e.g., galleries, lobbies, classrooms, lunchrooms) are programmable, and management has decided how every public space will be programmed all year. A programmable museum seeks to achieve its purposes by operating its yearly selection of programs.

My suggestion is to apply this process more broadly and to focus a museum's resources on producing programs, each of which is planned to serve specific audiences under sustainable business models.

Of course, once I define *program* as any museum activity or offering, regardless of format, then museums can claim to have always been *programmable*, even if those programs were permanent installations of exhibits, art, or collections. True, but I hope museums use the term more actively—that a *programmable museum* changes its programs frequently using a mix of learning styles to engage a diversity of audiences in a variety of cultural contexts and locations over time.

NEXT STEPS

These chapters are not implementation blueprints. Instead, they rethink some museum practices and propose suggestions to consider. Some of you may be making these changes already, others may find the degree of change daunting. Each chapter could be a book on its own, but my goal is to share these suggestions at the introductory level and to describe their potential benefits.

Talk about the ideas among your colleagues. Which ones address your current situation and needs? Which ones might be low-hanging fruit given your museum's need for nourishment? Choose an idea or two to try out at some scale, one step at a time.

But keep the big vision in mind. Let the worthy goals and full benefits motivate your progress. The small, first steps can be justified by the vision.

Most suggestions are disruptive; they aim to replace old systems in place. It may take time and work to implement some of them, but now may be the best, most effective time to make these changes.

I understand the devil is in the details, and the details are at your end. I have suggested directions and now urge you to rethink and unlearn any apparent obstacles. Your museum can choose the road map, the transport, and your fellow journeyers.

All my suggestions share a goal: to help you make your museum more effective at achieving the impacts you desire.

NOTE

1. https://www.aam-us.org/2020/11/17/national-snapshot-of-covid-19/, accessed March 31, 2022.

Index

About the Author

John W. Jacobsen led museum analysis and planning for White Oak Associates, Inc., for more than forty years and over a hundred museums through hundreds of commissions. Projects include eighteen museums representing more than $1 billion of actual and anticipated investment in new and expanding museums internationally. In the 1980s, he was associate director of the Museum of Science in Boston. In 1988, the museum served 2.2 million visitors, an unsurpassed record. White Oak integrated operating economics with creative concepts in its plans.

Jacobsen's early career was in the theater, designing scenery or lighting for more than sixty shows from summer stock to regional theater to Broadway. This training led to producing educational sound-and-light shows internationally, before segueing to museums and their theaters.

Long committed to the museum field, Jacobsen is a founder of the Museum Film Network (1985), the Planetarium Show Network (1988), the Ocean Film Network (1992), AAM's Professional Committee on Green Museums (PIC Green 2008), and the Digital Immersive Giant Screen Specifications (DIGSS 1.0 2011). With Jeanie Stahl, Jacobsen formed the White Oak Institute in 2007, a nonprofit dedicated to research-based museum innovation, with completed awards and contracts with the National Science Foundation (NSF), the Institute of Museum and Library Services (IMLS), the American Alliance of Museums (AAM), and the Association of Children's Museums (ACM) to develop field-wide standards and data collection fields.

Jacobsen's extensive writings and presentations on museum topics have appeared in *Curator, Museum Management and Curatorship, Informal Learning Review*, and at AAM, ASTC, ACM, and other conferences. He is the author of *Measuring Museum Impact and Performance* (2016) and editor and coauthor of *The Museum Manager's Compendium* (2017), both published by Rowman & Littlefield. Jacobsen's BA and MFA are from Yale University.